Famous Biographies for Young People

FAMOUS BRITISH
WOMEN NOVELISTS

by Norah Smaridge

ILLUSTRATED WITH PHOTOGRAPHS

Dodd, Mead & Company · New York

FOR REGINA SMARIDGE

THE AUTHOR wishes to thank Miss Laurie Crisp and Miss Hilda Hunter for their kind help in locating source material.

Library of Congress Catalog Card Number: 67-22722
Printed in the United States of America
by Vail-Ballou Press, Inc., Binghamton, N.Y.

Thanks are due to the following for permission to reprint the material indicated:

Barnes & Noble, Inc.: for extracts from their Book Note guides of Jane Austen's *Emma* and George Eliot's *Middlemarch*, prepared by Norah Smaridge.

Jonathan Cape Ltd.: for extracts from *Mary Webb: Her Life and Work* by Thomas Moult.

The Viking Press, Inc.: for extracts from *Two Under the Indian Sun* by Jon and Rumer Godden. Copyright © 1966 by Jon and Rumer Godden.

Atheneum Publishers: for extracts from *Harold Nicolson: Diaries and Letters 1930–1939*, edited by Nigel Nicolson. Copyright © 1966 by William Collins Sons & Co., Ltd. Copyright © 1966 by Sir Harold Nicolson. Copyright © 1966 by Nigel Nicolson.

A. Watkins, Inc.: for extracts from the following works by Dorothy Sayers. *Have His Carcase;* Copyright 1932 by Dorothy Leigh Sayers Fleming. *Gaudy Night;* Copyright 1936 by Dorothy L. Sayers Fleming. *The Nine Taylors;* Copyright 1934.

-WI

CONTENTS

FANNY BURNEY

[1752–1840]

IN ALL OTHER respects a model young woman of her century, Fanny Burney differed from her contemporaries in one startling instance; she dared to write a novel. In the mid-eighteenth century it was considered shocking enough for a well brought-up girl to read a novel; to write one was unthinkable. Did not the Royal Princesses set an example? Their Highnesses never even peeked at the romances which their ladies-in-waiting sighed over so pleasurably.

Fanny wrote her novel in the utmost secrecy. Brother Charles, disguised "so as to make him seem older," carried the manuscript to the publisher, and the book was brought out anonymously. Months after its appearance, when her stepmother spotted a copy and demanded, *"Evelina*—what's that, pray?" Fanny was "horribly frightened." When the truth came out, her sin was condoned—but only because by then her novel was a great success.

Frances Burney was born in 1752 in Lynn, Norfolk, where her father was a church organist. A distinguished teacher, Doctor Charles Burney was in demand among the county gentlefolk. He rode to his pupils' homes on his mare, Peggy, studying Italian in the saddle and preparing himself for his magnum opus, a *History of Music*. Charming and articulate,

7

with a genius for friendship, he eventually became the most fashionable professor of music in London.

Fanny's mother, Esther Sleepe, was London bred, the daughter of a Huguenot refugee. She brought her husband no dowry, but her influential relatives were of service in securing pupils for him.

In 1760, the family moved to London and settled in Poland Street, an ideal teaching center where, in a very short time, Doctor Burney "had hardly an hour that was not appropriated to some fair disciple." Esther Burney, accomplished and lively, took full charge of their four daughters and two sons.

The Burney children were attractive, and markedly intelligent—all except Fanny, who at eight could not say the alphabet. No one seems to have worried about her. Her mother "had no fear for Fanny." Her brother teased her amusedly, pretending to teach her to read from a book held upside down. Fanny was not made to share her elder sister's lessons; an intensely shy child, she stayed contentedly in the background, showing no promise of developing any of the family cleverness.

Appearances were deceptive. Fanny was precociously alert; she observed—and she missed nothing. "I recollect your reading with our dear mother all Pope's works and Pitt's *Aeneid*," she wrote in later years to her sister. "I learned from hearing you recite them, before—many years before—I read them myself."

A year after the move to Poland Street, Mrs. Burney died, and Fanny, then nine, mourned her with unchildlike intensity. Doctor Burney bore the blow stoically and showed good sense in his management of his brood. He made no change in their way of living. A confidential servant, long in the employ of the family, ran the household capably, while Burney encouraged his friends' wives to take a kindly interest in his motherless children.

Her father's distinguished friends contributed in a most effective way to Fanny's development. David Garrick, the actor, and his delightful wife, La Violetta, often dropped into the Burney home to amuse the children with imitations and impromptu performances. Often, too, they invited them to occupy Mrs. Garrick's private box at the theater. In his memoirs, Doctor Burney told how Fanny, after seeing a play, "used to take the actors off, and compose speeches for their characters, for she could not read them." Frequent contact with the Garricks stimulated Fanny's imagination, sharpened her ear for dialogue—and made her realize that she must learn to read and write if she wanted to compose plays of her own.

She set to work to educate herself. By the time she was eleven, she was scribbling epics, dramas, and stories, using her own brand of hieroglyphics. Allowed the run of her father's library, she read widely, usually in a spirit of criticism. But she preferred her own compositions; Fanny Burney was never to become a genuine book lover or develop a taste for literature.

Another of her father's friends, Samuel Crisp, became a "second Daddy" to the small girl. A man of the world, once wealthy and traveled but now in straitened circumstances, he had recently chosen to retire to Chessington Hall, a crumbling and almost inaccessible mansion that dated back to the time of Cardinal Wolsey. Here, with a friend of similar tastes, he led a hermit-like existence, occasionally emerging to enjoy the concerts and art exhibitions of the London season.

Fanny and her father often visited Crisp, and she always replied in full to the long letters he wrote her—letters that were a running commentary on life, literature and art. From Crisp, Fanny learned the priceless gift of writing naturally, not imitatively or with eighteenth-century affectation.

When Fanny was fifteen, her father married Elizabeth Allen, a widow with children of her own. A handsome, well-educated woman, she proved to be an excellent stepmother and an admirable wife. Unwittingly, she did Fanny a great service when, disapproving of girls who "scribbled," she warned her not to waste her time in "idle inventions." The docile Fanny promptly made a bonfire of her juvenilia; this acted as a refining agency so that only the most worthwhile of her compositions persisted in her memory. These included a sentimental tale of the adventures of a young lady named Caroline Evelyn.

She could not forget her heroine. In the years that followed, she plotted and replotted the story, always to its advantage; as a result, every character and incident in *Evelina* was perfectly shaped long before she put a line on paper.

When she began the actual writing, Fanny swore her brothers and sisters to secrecy. She wrote surreptitiously; then in her early twenties, she had little time or privacy. As her father's willing amanuensis, she spent much of her time making fair copies of his musical works. As a daughter of the house, she had to help entertain the parade of visitors—Sir Joshua Reynolds; Edmund Burke; the sculptor Nollekens; Bruce, the Abyssinian traveler; and Omai, the "gentle savage" of Cowper's poem. The famous Doctor Johnson was an honored guest, though apt to be disconcerting; he once opened a volume of the encyclopedia, lost himself in its pages, and forgot the company who had come to hear him talk.

By the time she had finished two volumes of *Evelina*, Fanny began to weary of it. Naïvely, she wrote Dodsley, a well-known bookseller, "a letter of mysterious character, unsigned, inquiring if he would be prepared to consider publication of two volumes of the work immediately, and the remainder after a lapse of a year." Dodley refused but Lowndes, an enterprising publisher, expressed interest in the book although he would not promise publication until he had seen the third volume.

Fanny took a year to complete *Evelina*. Then, choosing the moment when he was leaving for a visit to Chessington Hall, she asked her father's permission to publish "a little book" she had written. Surprised and amused, Doctor Burney gave his consent and, as Fanny had hoped, forgot the matter completely.

Evelina was published in January of 1778, and by the end of May two editions had been exhausted. Fanny kept her secret cleverly; letters from her publisher were mailed to the Orange Coffee House, where Brother Charles picked them up. However, when she was convalescing at Chessington Hall after an attack of inflammation of the lungs, Fanny could not resist reading *Evelina* to Daddy Crisp and hinting mysteriously at its authorship.

Meantime, *Evelina* was the subject of excited speculation in the drawing-rooms of such fashionable ladies as Mrs. Cholmondely, who declared she would keep the book on her table all summer "to make it as widely known as possible." Her rival, Mrs. Thrale, an indefatigable hostess, "fell into a rapture" over *Evelina* and passed it on to Doctor Johnson, who gobbled it up, volume after volume. Sir Joshua Reynolds forgot his dinner as he read it, and Edmund Burke sat up all night to finish it.

The book had been published for six months before Doctor Burney, who had ordered a copy for himself, discovered that the dedicatory Ode was addressed to himself. "How great must have been his astonishment at seeing himself so addressed!" Fanny observed in her *Diary*. "Indeed, Charlotte says he looked all amazement, read a line or two with great eagerness, and then, stopping short, he seemed quite affected, and the tears started into his eyes."

There was a merry scene with Daddy Crisp, whom Fanny feared to face after her deception was discovered. She need not have worried. "He caught both my hands," she told her *Diary*, "and looked as if he would have looked me through, and then exclaimed, 'Why, you little hussy—you young devil—aren't you ashamed to look me in the face, you *Evelina* you! Why, what a dance you have led me about it! Young friend, indeed! Oh, you little hussy! What tricks you have served me!'"

With every reason for showing Fanny off, Doctor Burney now took her to meet Mrs. Thrale, whom Fanny described to her sister as "the goddess of my idolatry." The two women took to each other at once and Fanny began to spend much of her time with this new friend.

For the next six years, Fanny moved in fashionable society under the wing of Mrs. Thrale, meeting such literary giants as Richard Brinsley Sheridan, who suggested that she should try her hand at writing a comedy. Flattered, Fanny set to work on *The Witlings*, an imitative comedy which, as Daddy Crisp foresaw, was not a success.

Fanny took the disappointment philosophically; she was already at work on her second novel, *Cecilia*, although its progress was slowed by trips to Bath, Brighton, and elsewhere with Mrs. Thrale. When Mrs. Thrale's husband died, Fanny laid the book aside in order to devote all her time and thought to the widow.

When it finally appeared, four years after *Evelina*, *Cecilia* was enthusiastically received. "My eyes red with reading and crying, I stop every moment to kiss the book and wish it were my Burney!" Mrs. Thrale exclaimed as she read it. "'Tis the sweetest book, the most interesting, the most engaging. Oh! it beats every other book, even your own other volume. *Evelina* was a baby to it."

Actually, *Cecilia* is far inferior to *Evelina*. Fanny was no longer writing naturally and spontaneously. Influenced by her admiration for Doctor Johnson, she unconsciously mimicked his style. *Cecilia* is labored, unreal, and—to the twentieth century—unreadable.

To her father's consternation, Fanny wrote nothing during the next three years; preoccupied with her ever-widening circle of friends and acquaintances, she was not even thinking of writing. She had sad preoccupations, too; Daddy Crisp died in 1783, and Fanny, "the dearest thing to him on earth," was with him during his last days. Doctor Johnson, too, was in failing health, and when Fanny saw him in November, 1784, it was for the last time.

She suffered another shock when, in the summer of that year, Mrs. Thrale made what her friends considered an ill-advised marriage with an inoffensive little singing teacher called Piozzi. Opposed to the union, Fanny was unable to congratulate her friend with any warmth. The new Mrs. Piozzi was hurt and chagrined, and the friendship and correspondence of six years came to an abrupt end.

Mrs. Thrale's place in Fanny's affections was taken by a new friend, an elderly woman, Mrs. Delaney, intimate friend of the Dowager Duchess of Portland and a great favorite of the King and Queen. For two years, Fanny visited Mrs. Delaney every week, either in her London house or in the summer cottage, close to Windsor Castle, which the King himself had equipped for her.

It was largely through Mrs. Delaney's influence that Fanny received a visit from a Mr. Smelt, commissioned by the Queen to make her an offer. The office of keeper of the robes, he explained, was jointly held by two Germans, who had accompanied Charlotte of Mecklenburg-Strelitz when she came to England. One of these ladies was retiring—and Miss Burney was invited to take her place.

Doctor Burney was awed—and relieved. He had been worrying about his spinster daughter, now thirty-four and without a suitor in sight. He was sixty years of age himself, and he had saved very little money. What was to become of Fanny if, as looked likely, she did not return to her writing? Not unnaturally, he believed that acceptance of the offer would be greatly to Fanny's advantage.

Fanny herself was aghast at the idea; to take a post with the Queen was tantamount to retiring into a convent. "The attendance was to be incessant," she wrote to a friend, "the confinement to the court continual; I was scarce ever to be spared for a single visit from the palaces, nor to receive anybody but with permission; and what a life for me, who have friends so dear to me, and to whom friendship is the balm, the comfort, the very support of existence!"

Nevertheless, she let herself be persuaded by her father, by unthinking friends, and by an interview during which the Queen said "with the most condescending softness, 'I am sure, Miss Burney, we shall suit one another very well.'" Apprehensive, but yielding with good grace, Fanny was soon installed in her own apartments in the Queen's Lodge.

It was a wretched mistake. Puny, short-sighted, extremely nervous, Fanny was totally unfitted to be a lady-in-attendance. Summarizing her round of duties in her journal, she wrote with a kind of desperation ". . . the early rising, and a long day's attention to new affairs and occupations, cause a fatigue so bodily that nothing mental stands against it, and to sleep I fall the moment I have put out my candle and laid down my head."

Her duties were not really arduous; she had to attend the

queen's toilet, take care of her lap dog—and mix her snuff. Together with her senior, Mrs. Schwellenberg, she had to entertain the King's equerries and any visitors who might be waiting to see him. But, for Fanny, the days were a purgatory; she was a prisoner, never alone, unable to do, without permission, any of the things which she had always done freely.

Unbearable though they were for Fanny, her five years as Second Keeper of the Robes were to prove a rich source of entertainment and information for her readers. The journal of her life at court is a rich gallery of personnages, made living and immediate by her facile pen. Because of Fanny's powers of observation, Queen Charlotte and King George are better known to us than any royal pair mentioned in English history.

The reader must go to Fanny's famous *Diary* for a day-by-day account of her doings: the trips she took, in attendance on the Queen, to country houses so large that she roamed the passages like a ghost, unable to find her room; the banquets at which she was an onlooker, faint with hunger; the bullying she endured from Mrs. Schwellenberg, "a peevish old person of uncertain temper and impaired health, swaddled in the buckram of backstairs etiquette."

The strain of those years, with their irksome duties and deadly monotony, told on Fanny's health. Early in 1791, when her friends spotted Fanny in the royal entourage at Windsor or Kew, they were aghast at the change in her. James Boswell, meeting her one morning at the church gate of St. George's Chapel, asked with blunt indignation, "My dear ma'am, why do you stay?—it won't do, ma'am! you must resign!—we can put up with it no longer. I told my good host the bishop so last night; we are all grown quite outrageous!"

Urged on by his daughter's protesting friends, Doctor

Burney, together with Fanny, prepared a memorial which she presented to the Queen, asking permission to resign. Although the Queen "betrayed a blank disappointment," she not only gave her consent but allowed Fanny a retiring pension of a hundred pounds a year.

Wan and thin, Fanny returned to her father's house in Chelsea. After three weeks, she set out on a tour of southwest England, revisiting Bath and the scenes of her former happiness. When the end of the holiday approached, her father wrote to her eagerly: "The great grubbery will be in nice order for you, as well as the little; both have lately had many accessions of new books. The ink is good, good pens in plenty, and the most pleasant and smooth paper in the world."

Almost restored to health, Fanny set to work eagerly—but not on the novel for which her readers had been waiting. For three years, by fits and starts, she worked on three tragedies. At the end of that time the first one was produced, and failed. Fanny Burney's genius was not for tragedy.

In 1792, she became acquainted with a group of French exiles who had taken a house close to her sister's. All were accomplished and agreeable, but one in particular, Monsieur Alexandre d'Arblay, was irresistible to Fanny. "M. d'Arblay," she wrote, "is one of the most singularly interesting characters that can ever have been formed. He has a sincerity, an ingenuous openness of nature that I have been unjust enough to think could not belong to a Frenchman."

Now on the verge of forty-one, Fanny outdid her own heroines; in spite of her father's disapproval, she married this alien and penniless ex-brigadier and settled down to love in a cottage—a laborer's cottage, "with a garden of cabbages, potatoes and asparagus, the last named being, in an excess of zeal, rooted up as a weed by the soldier whose sword had been turned into a pruninghook."

The marriage was eminently happy and was blessed with a son, baptized Alexandre Charles Louis Piochard, in 1794. Contentment sent Fanny back to her writing desk. This time she took two years to finish a novel, *Camilla*, which was published by subscription. Edmund Burke sent her twenty guineas for a set of volumes and Queen Charlotte, to whom the book was dedicated, gave her a hundred guineas from herself and the King.

Dull and pedantic as the novel seems to modern readers, it was a success in Fanny's time. Out of the proceeds, three thousand pounds, the D'Arblays built a small house, Camilla Cottage, where they lived in modest comfort until 1801. Then Fanny accompanied her husband to France, where he hoped to recover his confiscated property or be given lucrative employment. All he received, however, was a tiny "retiring income" and a humble position as a government clerk.

For more than ten years, the D'Arblays lived in suburban Passy, received in the best Parisian circles in spite of their near poverty. Then, eager to send her son to study at Cambridge University, Fanny paid a visit to England. Here she wrote *The Wanderer*, a novel in five volumes, published in 1814. In that same year, her father died at the age of eighty-six.

A few days after his death, Fanny was a little heartened by her presentation to King Louis XVIII. Addressing her "in very pretty English," he told of his delight in her novels. Within a few weeks, she heard the glad news that her husband was to receive a commission in the king's Corps de Garde. She and Alexandre celebrated by paying a fleeting visit to England, where they left their son behind to continue his studies at Cambridge.

Back in France, the D'Arblays had to flee to Belgium; Napoleon, escaped from Elba, had entered Paris, putting the

King to flight. In Brussels with thousands of other refugees, Fanny waited for the crisis—the Battle of Waterloo. Her account of Waterloo week is so vivid that writers as famous as Thackeray drew upon it for the background of their novels. Although Fanny's novels had deteriorated in style, becoming labored and affected, her *Diary* was written with complete naturalness and spontaneity.

Misfortune continued to dog Alexandre d'Arblay. Just when he might well expect a reward for his years of service, he was kicked by a horse and so disabled that he had to retire from active service. Three years later, he died in Bath.

The grieving Fanny still had twenty-two years ahead of her—quiet and eventless years which she spent in London, devoting herself to compiling her fathers *Memoirs*. On November 18, 1826, she was visited by Sir Walter Scott, who left this record in his *Diary*.

"Introduced to Madame d'Arblay, the celebrated authoress of *Evelina* and *Cecilia*, an elderly lady with no remains of personal beauty, but with a simple and gentle manner, a pleasing expression of countenance, and apparently quick feelings. . . . I trust I shall see this lady again."

In January, 1837, Fanny's son, Alexandre, died of influenza. He had graduated from Cambridge University, taken orders, and was planning to marry. His mother survived him for nearly three years, dying after a severe illness made harrowing by delusions.

Forerunner of those nineteenth-century women novelists who contributed such enduring works to English literature, Fanny wielded great influence in her day. She not only gave us *Evelina* and *Cecilia*, as well as less meritorious novels, but inspired such masterpieces as Maria Edgeworth's *The Absentees* and Jane Austen's *Mansfield Park*.

In her novels, as in her *Diary*, Fanny Burney was "very

much a lady," lively, witty, and observant, but always deco-
rous and discreet. Daring to write at a time when novel reading for young ladies was frowned upon, she wrote with such
taste and delicacy that her books "made the circulating
library respectable." Even princesses might read Fanny Burney. When the D'Arblays paid a visit to court to present a
copy of *Camilla* to Queen Charlotte, Princess Elizabeth cried
out, "I've got leave! And Mama says she won't wait to read it
first!" By which that royal young lady meant that she had
obtained permission to read *Camilla* without even having to
wait for it to be censored in advance by her mother.

JANE AUSTEN

[1775–1817]

ONE OF THE most perceptive and delightful writers of English fiction, Jane Austen was born into the sheltered world of a country parsonage, near Basingstoke, Hampshire, on December 16, 1775. Steventon, her home for twenty-five years, was "tolerably roomy and commodious," even for a family with seven children and dozens of friends and acquaintances. It had a walled garden, strawberry beds to plunder, a "wood walk" overhung by tall elms, and a sundial to mark agreeable hours in which nothing unexpected ever happened.

Jane was blessed in her parents. George Austen was a man of superior intellect and excellent education, who gained a scholarship to St. John's, Oxford, and became a Fellow of his college. He was well able to direct his daughters' studies and prepare his sons for the university. Jane's mother, Cassandra, was a slight, handsome, spirited woman, with a talent for writing sparkling letters and gay but commonsensible verse. Something of an individualist, she usually dressed in a riding habit of scarlet cloth, which was later cut down to make trousers for her sons.

Although she was devoted to her brothers, Jane was most attached to her sister, Cassandra, her elder by three years. When Cassandra was sent to boarding school, Jane went too;

she was young for formal schooling but she would have been wretched without her sister. "If Cassandra were going to have her head cut off," their mother observed, "Jane would insist on sharing her fate."

Their five brothers wielded a good deal of influence over the girls. James, the eldest, well read in English literature, helped to form Jane's reading taste. Edward, who made their childhood merry, left a sad gap when he was adopted by wealthy cousins and left Steventon forever. Henry, less successful than the other Austens, resided in London at one period of his life and was thus able to transact necessary business with Jane's publisher.

The two youngest brothers brought vicarious adventure into Jane's life. Francis and Charles both saw action in the British Navy, rose to be admirals, and carried their flags to distant stations. Francis, who reached the very summit of his profession, becoming Senior Admiral of the Fleet, may have stood for the Edward Price of *Mansfield Park* as well as for the Captain Wentworth or the Admiral Crofton of *Persuasion*. Her seagoing brothers made Jane very knowledgeable about ships and sailors; she followed every step of their lives, devouring their letters and poring over the gifts and souvenirs which they brought home. No flaw has ever been detected in her seamanship, either in *Mansfield Park* or *Emma*.

For the most part, Jane and Cassandra were educated at home. Higher education for women was not usual at that time, and the Austen girls were no better instructed than other young ladies of their day. Jane was especially skilled at needlework, in which she delighted. She was no artist, and only moderately musical; like her heroine, Elizabeth Bennett, "her performance was pleasing though by no means capital." She was an excellent French scholar and a fair Italian one.

Though it pleased her to call herself "ignorant and un-

informed," and though she declared that she hated solid reading, Jane was well acquainted with the standard authors of
her time and had a fair knowledge of English literature.
Crabbe, Cowper, Johnson, and Scott were her favorite poets,
though she set Crabbe highest. It was a joke in the family that
she would have been delighted to become Mrs. Crabbe if she
had ever been personally acquainted with the poet.

Jane had at least one brief but happy experience of school
life. Like their aunts before them, she and Cassandra were sent
to the Abbey School, adjoining the remains of the ancient
Abbey of Reading. Discipline seems to have been relaxed,
because the girls, with their cousin, Emily Cooper, were permitted to accept an invitation to supper at the local inn with
Edward Austen and Edward Cooper. The Abbey School,
lingering in Jane's memory, no doubt served as the model for
Mrs. Goddard's school in *Emma*. It was "a real, honest, old-
fashioned Boarding-school, where a reasonable amount of
accomplishments were sold at a reasonable price, and where
girls might be sent to be out of the way, and scramble themselves into a little education without any danger of coming
back prodigies." From an artificial embankment in the beautiful old garden, the students could look down on the magnificent ruins of a church begun by Henry I and consecrated
by Becket in 1125. The abbey, with its past history and its
relics of ancient grandeur, may well have impressed the child
Jane and later suggested some of the features of her own
Northanger Abbey.

The future novelist grew up in an atmosphere of encouragement and approval. She was the darling of her home, and
nothing she wrote was ever unkindly scrutinized. How soon
she began to produce finished stories is not certain, but from a
very early age her writings were a source of amusement and
interest to her family. When she was about twelve, the young

Austens developed a craze for private theatricals, and Jane kept them supplied with plays of her own composition.

Some of her copybooks, still extant, contain tales and dramas written before she was sixteen. Dedicated with mock solemnity to some member of her family, they poke sly fun at the grandiloquent dedications then in fashion. Before long, her stories became burlesques of the sentimental romances and wildly improbable horror tales of the day. "She seemed to be teaching herself how NOT to write," says one of her biographers. Jane's contempt for the state of mind that expected a mystery in everything was later shown in the incident in *Northanger Abbey*, when Catherine Morland, fired with curiosity, pulls out a bundle of dusty papers from an ancient cabinet, only to find them to be a roll of laundry bills.

The passing years brought few changes to the family in Steventon Parsonage. James, Edward, and Henry all made their start in life, and the two eldest ones married. Francis and Charles went into the Navy. Cassandra took her place as the "Miss Austen" of the family, and finally it became Jane's turn to be, as she wrote to a friend, "grown up and have a fine complexion, and wear great square muslin shawls."

During the last five years of her life at Steventon, Jane wrote long and consistently. At least three of her best-known novels, *Pride and Prejudice*, *Sense and Sensibility*, and *Northanger Abbey*, were written during this period. It is difficult to understand how she managed to combine so much literary work with all her household and social occupations, and she herself sheds no light on the subject. She writes to Cassandra, when her sister is away visiting, and tells her the smallest details of home happenings—without once mentioning the subject of her writing. It cannot have been from shyness, because her family knew of her activities and the actual writing was done in the family sitting room.

However, there was still prejudice against women writers, so Jane was careful to keep her work a secret from the outside world. Callers at the parsonage were apt to find her doing embroidery or playing spillikins or cup and ball. They seldom saw her at her desk. Jane, ingenious, contrived to do her writing on small scraps of paper which could easily be put away or covered with a piece of needlework.

Pride and Prejudice was the first of her novels to be completed. She began it in October, 1796, when she was twenty-one, and finished it ten months later. Her father, anxious to judge it fairly, set himself a course of reading in the contemporary novel. Six months later, he read his daughter's work and was certain of its quality. He at once wrote to Cadell, an eminent London publisher, offering to send the novel for consideration. The refusal was so definite and so chilling that the manuscript was laid away in an attic, where it remained for eleven years.

Jane's philosophic disposition was proof against disappointment. She was already at work on *Sense and Sensibility*. *Northanger Abbey*, composed in the following year, completed the trio of novels written at Steventon.

Northanger Abbey found a purchaser when, in 1798, Jane sold the manuscript, again anonymously, to Crosbie and Company of London for a modest ten pounds. The publisher, not realizing its value, locked it in a safe for several years and made no attempt to put it in print.

No one in the neighborhood suspected that there was "a chiel amang them, takin' notes." Jane appeared to be pleasantly occupied with domestic duties and social life. Her parents were comfortably off; they had neighbors and cousins to entertain and visit. They kept a carriage and a pair of horses, although Jane and her sister sometimes trudged in pattens through the muddy roads to call on their friends in the adjoining parish of Ashe.

Jane was always ready for a game of commerce or lottery, for an occasional dance or a trip to Bath to see her cousins. Sir Eddgerton Brydges says in his autobiography: "When I knew Jane Austen, I never suspected that she was an authoress, but my eyes told me that she was fair and handsome, slight and elegant, but with cheeks a little too full." Jane's nephew echoed him later. "In person, Jane Austen was very attractive. Her figure was rather tall and slender, her step firm and light, and her whole appearance expressive of health and animation. In complexion, she was a clear brunette with a rich colour; she had full, round cheeks, with mouth and nose small and well formed, bright hazel eyes, and brown hair forming natural curls round her face. If not so regularly handsome as her sister, yet her countenance had a peculiar charm of its own."

Attractive though she was, Jane seems to have had no serious romance. Her family declared that she was heart-whole, but there were passing fancies. She continued to be devoted to her sister, especially after the tragic ending to Cassandra's love affair. The young clergyman to whom she was engaged, not being rich enough to marry, went out to the West Indies as chaplain to a regiment. He caught yellow fever on his arrival, and died in a few days.

Settling, of her own choice, into spinsterhood, Jane soon took to wearing caps, the symbol of middle age. In a sketch made by Cassandra, she is shown in a small, quilted tulle cap. Short round curls shade her forehead, and her expression is arch, intelligent, and lively. She seems to be wide awake to everything that is going on around her, finding it a source of considerable amusement.

The first great change in Jane's life came in 1801 when her father, in failing health, confided the living of Steventon to his son and moved to Bath with his wife and daughters. At first the thought of such a move was disturbing. But Jane, a determined optimist, was soon writing cheerfully to her sister: "I am becoming more and more reconciled to the idea of departure. We have lived long enough in this neighbourhood; the Basingstoke balls are certainly on the decline; there is something interesting in the bustle of going away, and the prospect of spending future summers by the sea or in Wales is delightful." As Cassandra was away on a visit, and their mother was in delicate health, it was left to Jane to cope with the problems of transportation and house hunting.

She managed well. "Our journey was perfectly free from accident or event," she wrote to Cassandra. "We had charming weather, hardly any dust, and were exceedingly agreeable as we did not speak above once in three miles. We had a very neat chaise from Devizes; it looked almost as well as a gentleman's, at least as a very shabby gentleman's. . . . We drank tea as soon as we arrived; and so ends the account of our journey, which my mother bore without any fatigue."

Until they found a house, they stayed with Mrs. Austen's married sister, Mrs. Leigh Perrot, and settled down to the staid routine of life in a spa. Bath was not new to Jane Austen, but its heyday, as described by her in *Northanger Abbey*, was now over. The sleepy town suited her parents, but Jane found its small gaieties uninspiring. "Another stupid party last night," she wrote to her sister. "Perhaps if larger they might be less intolerable, but here there were only just enough to make one card table, with six people to look on and talk nonsense to each other."

Perhaps she found Bath too stultifying. Perhaps she was too preoccupied with her parents' health. Whatever the cause, she composed nothing of importance while she was there. She began only one story, the tale of a girl of natural refinement early taken away from a vulgar home and placed among cultivated people. But she did not finish it or even divide it into chapters. When she left Bath in 1805, she had nothing but this fragment to add to the valuable stock of writing which she had brought with her from Steventon.

After the death of Mr. Austen in 1805, his widow and daughters moved to Southampton, where a friend of Jane's, Martha Lloyd, came to live with them and was a great source of happiness to the little family. Their house was pleasant enough, with a garden for Mrs. Austen's enjoyment, but the Austens never took root there. Jane felt as little at home as she had in Bath, and wrote nothing during their stay.

When an opportunity of escape was offered, they took it eagerly. Edward, now a wealthy and landed gentleman, offered them the choice of two estates—Godmersham Park, in Kent, and Chawton Cottage, in Hampshire. They chose the latter, a small house which was altered and fitted up to suit the four ladies. Jane settled in happily, little knowing that this was to be her last home.

Chawton Cottage was a fair-sized house, fronting upon the road, but with the sitting rooms so located that they looked out upon the garden. Edward Austen had planted trees and shrubs, and thrown together two or three small fields where the ladies could take the gentle walks which were their only exercise. Anything more vigorous would have been frowned upon; Elizabeth Bennett, in *Pride and Prejudice*, was sneered at for walking six miles across country.

The house was large enough for entertaining, and the Austens had many callers, friends and relatives in the neighborhood whom they took pleasure in meeting as often as they could. The brothers and their families were frequent visitors, and all the young nephews and nieces looked upon a visit to "Aunt Jane" as a delightful privilege. "As a very small girl, I was always creeping up to Aunt Jane," a niece wrote after Jane's death, "and following her whenever I could, in the house and out of it. . . . She could make everything amusing to a child."

Settled in a real home again, Jane returned to her writing. Now she was working in the most pleasant of environments and under the best possible circumstances. She had the continual companionship of Cassandra, the uncritical admiration of Martha Lloyd, and the country life that she delighted to share and observe. She could give herself fully to the kind of literary life which was second nature to her.

In the summer of 1811, two years after the move to Chawton Cottage, Jane at last saw publication. *Sense and Sensibility* was at once appreciated by the public, and Jane, at thirty-six, was firmly launched on a career of authorship. But she was so modest and her expectations were so humble that she saved something out of her income to meet any possible loss over the publication of her novel. When she learned that the book had made a hundred and fifty pounds for her, she was surprised and gratified, remarking that it was a great deal to earn for so little trouble.

The success of *Sense and Sensibility* encouraged Jane to submit *Pride and Prejudice* to her publisher, and it appeared in 1813. "I feel I must write to you today," she told Cassandra. "I want to tell you that I have got my own darling child from London." Her own opinion of the heroine followed. "I must confess that I think her (Elizabeth) as delightful a creature as ever appeared in print, and how I shall be able to tolerate those who do not like *her* at least, I do not know."

Mansfield Park, the first of the novels written at Chawton, placed Jane Austen in the first rank of English writers. Twelve years of observation, of lying fallow, had borne rich fruit; Jane's work had gained in depth, in subtlety, and in variety. The theatricals at Mansfield Park, the hopes and doubts of the amateur actors, and busy, meddling Mrs. Norris are presented as only Jane could present them. Languid Lady Bertram is one of those commonplace persons whom ordinary novelists despair of infusing with life. Fanny Price, the poor relation in a great family, is far more interesting than Jane herself realized; her own favorite is Elizabeth, in *Pride and Prejudice*.

After the publication of *Mansfield Park*, Jane began to fear that she might be written out, but the gallery of portraits in her next novel, *Emma*, shows no falling off. She gives us such creations as the simple-minded Mr. Woodhouse; Mrs. Elton, the bride, eager to patronize everyone; the voluble Miss Bates, pleased with everything, alike delighted by the hindquarter of pork, her niece Jane, and the rivet in her mother's spectacles.

Though she found her inspiration in the people around her, none of Jane's acquaintances ever accused her of "putting them in a book." She took note of peculiarities, weaknesses, affectations in speech and manners, but her characters are her own inventions. "I am too proud of my gentlemen to admit that they were only Mr. A., or Colonel B.," she once said. Her own favorite heroes were Edmund Bertram and Emma's Mr. Knightley, but she modestly declared that they were far from being adequate portraits of English gentlemen.

After the warm reception given to her novels by the public, it occurred to Jane and her family that it might be well to rescue *Northanger Abbey* from its unappreciative purchaser, who was still in no hurry to publish it. Her brother Henry undertook the negotiations and succeeded in getting the manuscript back for the same price that was paid for it. Both parties to the bargain were satisfied, but the publisher would have felt very differently if he had realized that the book was written by one of the most popular authors of the day. The book was published posthumously in 1818.

Persuasion, the last of Jane Austen's novels, was finished in August, 1816, but was not published until after her death. It shows her at the peak of her powers. The families of Eliots, Musgroves, and Crofts, the little interests of Bath life, and the returning affection of Captain Wentworth for his former love, Anne Eliot, are touched with all the liveliness and delicacy which make Jane Austen's novels incomparable.

But as she was writing the final chapters, Jane fell ill. Gradually, she grew weaker. With typical unselfishness, she rejected the sofa in the family living room, which was tacitly reserved for Mrs. Austen, now over seventy. Instead, she contrived a sofa out of two chairs, which she declared to be more comfortable than a real one.

As spring came on, Jane went to Winchester to be near her doctor, but he was unable to do anything to help her. She accepted his verdict philosophically, and even managed to cheer and divert her family. To the last, she was more concerned with others than with herself. In a letter written just before her death, she hoped that Cassandra had not been made ill by her exertions. "As to what I owe her," she said, "and the anxious affection of all my beloved family on this occasion, I can only cry over it, and pray God to bless them more and more."

Jane Austen died peacefully on July 18, 1817, in her forty-second year. She was buried in Winchester Cathedral. Some years after her death, when a gentleman was visiting the cathedral, he asked to be shown Miss Austen's grave. "Pray, sir," the verger asked, "can you tell me whether there is anything remarkable about this lady? So many people want to know where she is buried."

Today there are few of her countrymen who have not heard of Jane Austen. She has become a classic. Fresh editions of her work are continually being issued. Her novels are enjoyed by thousands of readers who owe to her some of the happiest hours of their lives. Books are still being written about her, analyzing her art, her character, her personality. Twentieth-century authors G. B. Stern and Sheila Kaye-Smith found her inexhaustible; their protracted conversation about the inimitable Jane is the subject of two books, *Speaking of Jane Austen* and *More About Jane Austen*.

Thirty-five years after her death, Jane Austen received a tribute from the United States. The Quincy family of Boston, Massachusetts, wrote a charming letter to Sir Francis Austen, Jane's brother. In it, they explained that they had been introduced to Miss Austen's novels by the highest judicial authorities, including Mr. Chief Justice Marshall and his associate, Mr. Justice Story. "For many years, her talents have brightened our daily path," said the letter, "and her name and those of her characters are familiar to us as 'household words.' We have long wished to express to some of her family the sentiments of gratitude and affection she has inspired."

THE BRONTË SISTERS

CHARLOTTE [1816–1855]
EMILY JANE [1818–1848]
ANNE [1820–1849]

THE YEAR 1846 is a memorable one in the history of publishing; it saw the publication of Charlotte Brontë's *Jane Eyre*, Emily Brontë's *Wuthering Heights*, and Anne Brontë's *Agnes Grey*. The event of three sisters producing books of enduring worth in the same year is unique in literary history; so, too, is the interest which the sisters have excited ever since. With the sole exception of Shakespeare, they have produced more commentary than any other author.

Their lives were simple and tragically brief; it is their genius and personalities that defy easy analysis. From the beginning, the Brontës were unusual. When, as little children, they took possession of the room allotted to them in Haworth Parsonage, they christened it their "study," not their "nursery." The games they played in it were not childlike; nor were the reading and thinking they did there.

Charlotte, Emily, Anne, and their brother, Branwell, were born in the cramped parsonage at Thornton, near Bradford, in Yorkshire. There were already two older children, Maria and Elizabeth. In 1820, the family moved to Haworth, a lonely village on the edge of the wild moors. Although their new home looked like a palace to the children, Charlotte, a realist, had to agree with the little maid, Nancy, who dismissed their study with a contemptuous "Ye couldna swing a cat i' yon."

The parsonage was a bleak house, square and gray, with cold stone floors and uncurtained windows. Only sparse grass and a few straggling currant bushes grew in the neglected garden. Adjoining it was the churchyard, crowded with tombstones tilted crazily by wind and weather. At Haworth the children were on intimate terms with death. Funeral processions stumbled up the steep street to the church, and there were said to be graves even under the house.

Yet the Brontës loved Haworth. "I am home now," Charlotte wrote to her friend Ellen Nussey in later years, "and it feels like paradise." Emily, when exiled from her beloved moors, suffered a living death. Anne, twice governess in Yorkshire families, endured agonies of homesickness with gentle patience.

Their father, born Patrick Prunty, was one of ten children of a poor farmer in County Down, Ireland. High-spirited and ambitious, he left home when he was fifteen, opened a school, and made enough money to finance his education in England. After taking a degree at St. John's College, Cambridge, he was ordained a clergyman in the Church of England. By this time he had turned his back on his family; except for a lingering brogue, which later sat quaintly on the lips of his children, he showed no trace of his Irish blood. He changed his name to Brontë after hearing that Lord Nelson had been given a Sicilian dukedom of that name.

His wife, Maria Branwell, was a Cornishwoman, gentle and articulate. She was already ailing when they settled in the parsonage. Bedridden for the last months of her life, she shut herself away from her little ones, not wanting them to see her in pain. She died of cancer in 1821, her last words a cry of anguish, "Oh, God, my poor children."

Her death crushed her husband, putting an end to his purpose and ambition. From then on, Patrick Brontë secluded himself in his study to read, compose his sermons, whet his intellect on the political problems of the day—and develop a few eccentricities for which he did not apologize. "I do not deny that I am somewhat eccentrick," he wrote in later life to Mrs. Gaskell, who told some exaggerated and rather unkind stories about him in her biography of Charlotte. "Had I been numbered among the calm, sedate, concentric men of the world, I should not have been as I now am, and I should in all probability never have had such children as mine have been."

Self-centered though he was, Patrick was proud of his gifted progeny and provided for them as best he could. They, in return, were devoted to their father. True, he was often withdrawn, but he could, on occasion, be lively and talkative. A splendid raconteur, he would tell them tales of his Irish home, and even more thrilling yarns of the Yorkshire dales where the croppers, fearful of the newly invented machinery, combined into bands to fire the mills and attack the manufacturers.

Patrick did his best to find a second mother for his brood. Twice he proposed to his one-time sweetheart, Miss Mary Burden. Twice rejected, he resigned himself to the somewhat forbidding presence of his sister-in-law, Miss Branwell, who came from sunny Penzance to run the windswept parsonage.

Miss Branwell was both bad and good for the children. She had no gaiety, no tenderness, no deep love for them, but she was kind and conscientious. She did her duty by the girls; she taught them their first lessons, supervised their manners, and saw that they learned such domestic arts as cooking and sewing. More important, she left them free, making no emotional demands upon them. She never questioned what they did with their leisure; although she must often have noticed the growing pile of notebooks which they filled with stories, she did not attempt to direct or censor their writing. Nor did she grudge the affection they gave to Tabby, the blunt, warm-hearted Haworth woman who served the Brontës up to the last weeks of Charlotte's life, or the devotion which they lavished on animal pets—Emily's fierce mastiff, Keeper; Anne's spaniel, Flossy; and a number of kittens, canaries, hawks, and geese.

When a school for the daughters of impecunious clergy-men opened in nearby Cowan Bridge in 1824, Patrick Brontë at once despatched his two elder daughters. Two months later, he sent Charlotte and Emily to the same school, little knowing that Maria was suffering a kind of persecution at the hands of one of the teachers.

Whether the school authorities were as inhuman as Char-lotte later depicted them in *Jane Eyre* is unknown. Un-doubtedly, the site of the school was unhealthy, the building freezingly cold, the food scanty and tasteless. Maria, already delicate, fell ill, and the teachers failed to realize the serious-ness of that illness. When, alarmed, they at last sent for Mr. Brontë to take her home, it was too late; Maria died a few weeks after her return to Haworth. Her funeral was still fresh in the children's minds when Elizabeth, too, was brought home, to die of tuberculosis two weeks later. Shattered, Mr. Brontë sent for Charlotte and Emily, and for the next six years there was no further attempt to give the girls a formal education.

The double tragedy stunned the children, who felt the loss of Maria most keenly. Since her mother's death, she had tried to mother them herself; it was to Maria, rather than Aunt Branwell, that they had gone for sympathy or advice. Years later, Charlotte declared that Maria was the real genius of the Brontë family. Her father, with whom the little girl had begun to discuss politics on adult terms when she was only ten, described her as having "a powerfully intellectual mind."

Stepping into Maria's shoes, Charlotte began to dominate the others. Fiercely proud and loving, she was determined that they should educate themselves and make a name in the world. Following her lead, they eventually succeeded; with no relatives or friends, and with little attention from their father or Aunt Branwell, they began to develop their extraordinary gifts of intellect and imagination.

Emily, tall, graceful, and shy, was the most difficult to understand; her reserve and composure gave no clue to her ardent and indomitable nature. Anne, the prettiest of the three girls, moved in Emily's shadow; she, too, was silent by nature, but docile and gentle where Emily could be wild and rebellious. Branwell, their brother, was closest to Charlotte at the time; everything that the girls were not, he was—lively, brilliant, and so charming that even Aunt Branwell melted in his presence.

All four were insatiable readers, with an adult taste for the classics. Unlike most children of their day, they were allowed the run of the family bookshelf; they were also permitted to borrow books from the library at Ponden Hall, an Elizabethan house in the neighborhood. Though their tastes ranged far afield, they always returned to their favorites— Scott, Homer, Shakespeare, and the glittering fantasies of *The Arabian Nights*. Their appetite for tales of horror was easy to satisfy; Aunt Branwell's Methodist magazines offered spine-tingling stories of apparitions and nightmares.

The six years at home after the older girls' deaths were very important in the children's development. Physically, they remained surprisingly well, although their meager diet, the rain and snow during their moorland walks, and the air-lessness of their tiny study may well have been encouraging their latent tuberculosis. Mentally, they had excellent sustenance. Besides the books they owned and borrowed, they read five newspapers weekly and enjoyed spirited political arguments with their father and aunt.

Their creative life began when Mr. Brontë, returning from a visit to Leeds, brought home a box of wooden soldiers for Branwell. Charlotte, always a hero worshiper, pounced on one of them. "This is the Duke of Wellington!" she cried. "This shall be the Duke." Each chose and named a soldier and imaginations ran riot as they wove long and colorful stories of the doings of these heroes. From this beginning evolved their dream world, at first a single world which they shared together, and later a double world which they shared in pairs, Charlotte with Branwell, and Emily with Anne.

Unlike most daydreaming children, the Brontës put their dream worlds into writing. Charlotte and Branwell invented and directed the world of Angria, "a place of marble columns and rich draperies, of majestic mountains and stately rivers, of women dying for love and men always scornful, handsome and magniloquent." Emily and Anne fashioned a different world, Gondal, "a land of mist and moor and wild winds . . . a lane of stern, inexorable logic." In all, the Brontës wrote a hundred booklets, chronicles of Angria and Gondal, written in the minutest of script, on scraps of paper that were often less than two inches square. In time, these fantasies became more real to them than their own lives; they contributed immeasurably to the Brontës' development as writers but left them poorly equipped for the reality of the adult world which they were soon to enter.

In January, 1831, Charlotte was again sent away to school. This time, although she was often homesick, the experience was a happy one. Miss Wooler's school at Roe Head was small, pleasant, and beautifully situated. She herself became Charlotte's life-long friend. Charlotte excelled in her special subjects, literature, general knowledge, and drawing, and worked conscientiously and hard. She made two friends, Mary Taylor and Ellen Nussey, and when she returned to Haworth she began a correspondence with Ellen which lasted for years and shed valuable light on life in Haworth. "In the mornings," she wrote once, "from nine o'clock till half-past twelve, I instruct my sisters and draw; then we walk till dinner. After dinner I sew till tea-time, and after tea I either write, read, or do a little fancy-work, or draw, as I please."

In 1835, when Charlotte, her schooling finished, accepted an offer to return to Roe Head as a teacher, Emily was accepted as a pupil. But the formal teaching which so appealed to Charlotte held no attraction for Emily. Thin, pale, unhappy, she made no friends and pined for the moors. Fearing that her sister would die under such conditions, Charlotte saw to it that she returned home within six months.

Sheer force of character kept Charlotte herself at Roe Head. Temperamentally, she was unsuited to teaching. "Hard labour from six in the morning until eleven at night, with only one half-hour of exercise between. This is slavery," she wrote to a friend. At the end of six months, her health gave way, and the school's doctor ordered her home.

For a time, the Brontës were reunited. Except for their concern over Branwell, with whom failure had begun to be chronic, they were happy. Charlotte began to think about marriage, but recoiled indignantly when Ellen's brother, Henry Nussey, proposed to her; he was so obviously looking for a helpmate rather than a romance.

After a few months, she and Anne left home to be governesses, Anne with the kindly Ingham family, where she did her utmost to earn the children's love and respect, and Charlotte with the Sidgwick children, whom she soon found insupportable. On her return home she received her second proposal, a written declaration from a neighborhood curate, Mr. Bryce. As she had only met him once, she refused the offer wryly. "I am tolerably well convinced that I shall never marry at all," she wrote to Ellen Nussey. "Reason tells me so, and I am not so utterly the slave of feeling but that I can *occasionally hear* her voice."

By the summer of 1831, the Brontë girls had evolved a plan for living permanently in Haworth and running a school in the parsonage. First, though, it was decided that Charlotte and Emily should add to their accomplishments by a period of study abroad. For two years, the girls lived and studied in the Pensionnat Héger, a comfortable, well-run establishment in Brussels, where Charlotte found the life "delightful . . . so congenial to my own nature, compared with that of a governess."

Emily, although she worked diligently, was less impressed. She found it difficult to take direction from M. Héger, and she suffered cruelly from homesickness. On his side, M. Héger was full of admiration for his strong-minded pupil. "She should have been a man," he said, "a great navigator . . . her strong, imperious will could never have been daunted by opposition or difficulty; never have given way but with life."

Emily made no use of the Brussels experience in her later writing. Charlotte, more impressionable, used every facet of it in *The Professor* and *Villette;* she described the school in great detail and drew vivid but possibly exaggerated portraits of Monsieur and his wife.

Their Aunt Branwell's sudden death brought the girls back to Haworth, where Anne was waiting for them. For a time, they fell into their old routine. Then Anne returned to her position, and Branwell went to be tutor in the same family. Emily, now that the girls had received small legacies from Aunt Branwell, determined to stay at Haworth indefinitely: she would do the housework and be "happy and useful."

After some uncertainty, Charlotte accepted Madame Héger's invitation to return to Brussels as a teacher. But the experiment was not a success. She still disliked teaching, and she was lonely and depressed. M. Héger was the only person she wanted to confide in, and even he did not always understand her. Madame Héger began to spy on Charlotte, disapproving of her admiration for her husband. In December of 1844, longing for her home and family, Charlotte told the Hégers that she was leaving, and they did not press her to stay.

On her return to Haworth, Charlotte made feverish attempts to find pupils for their projected school, but none were forthcoming. "Everyone wishes us well," she observed, "but there are no pupils to be had." Emily dismissed the matter curtly; perhaps she was relieved that the privacy of Haworth was not to be invaded. "We did our little all," she said, "but it was no go."

In 1845, Charlotte made an astonishing discovery. Emily had been secretly writing poetry—poems that were "not at all like the poetry women generally write." Emily resented being found out, until Charlotte and Anne confessed that they, too, had been writing poems. Then she softened, and even let herself be persuaded to try her work for publication.

Hiding their identity, and at their own expense, the sisters brought out a slim volume, *Poems by Currer, Ellis and Acton Bell*. It sold badly, but the critics were kind and the *Westminster Review* found real genius in Emily's contribution. Although they were sick with worry over Branwell, who had become more and more dissipated and unstable as his sisters grew more disciplined and mature, they determined to become novelists. In the following months, each completed a book. Emily's *Wuthering Heights* and Anne's *Agnes Grey* were accepted at once, but Charlotte's *The Professor* was rejected as too slight in plot. With the publisher's encouragement, she began another novel, this time the melodramatic and deeply moving *Jane Eyre*. Rushed into print, it was published before the other two books and was an immediate success.

Wuthering Heights and *Agnes Grey* were not well received; the two books were shoddily produced in a single volume. Emily, stoical as usual, gave no clue to her feelings. Anne, patient and uncomplaining, set to work on her second book, *The Tenant of Wildfell Hall*. Charlotte, suffering for both of them, was outraged at what happened next. Anne's publisher, Newby, sold her new novel to America, claiming it to be a new work by the author of *Jane Eyre*.

Aghast, Charlotte decided that the sisters must reveal their identities. Overruling the objections of Emily and Anne, she conducted them to London, to the offices of her publishers, Smith, Elder. When the explanations were completed, Mr. Smith gave the sisters a royal time. They visited his family. They went to the opera. They stayed up unconscionably late. They left London loaded with books and returned to Haworth in a state of euphoria.

But their happiness came to an abrupt end. Branwell, his constitution shattered by dissipation, died soon after their return. "Nothing remains of him but a memory of errors and suffering," Charlotte wrote to a friend. "There is such a bitterness of pity for his life and death, such a yearning for the emptiness of his whole existence as I cannot describe."

There was worse to come. Emily, catching a chill at

Branwell's funeral, insisted on attending a memorial service—and never again went out of doors. Soon Charlotte was writing worriedly to Ellen Nussey: "Emily's cold and cough are very obstinate. I fear she has pain in the chest, and I sometimes catch a shortness in her breathing, when she has moved at all quickly. She looks very, very thin and pale. Her reserved nature occasions me great uneasiness of mind. It is useless to question her; you get no answers. It is still more useless to suggest remedies; they are never adopted."

Charlotte and Anne had the agony of watching Emily slowly die. Refusing sympathy, help, and medical care, she fought to stay on her feet. Even on the day of her death, she rose as usual at seven, dressed herself, and sat on the sofa, trying to sew. By noon, taking a turn for the worse, she managed to tell her sisters that she would see a doctor—but by then it was too late. She died a few hours later, on December 19, 1848.

Anne did not long survive her beloved sister. By Christmas, the terrified Charlotte was writing to Mr. Williams, her publisher's chief reader and her friend and literary confidant: "When we lost Emily, I thought we had drained the very dregs of our cup of trial, but now when I hear Anne cough as Emily coughed, I tremble lest there should be exquisite bitterness yet to taste."

Unlike Emily, Anne was tractable, obeying instructions and doing her pathetic best to live. At her own urging, Charlotte took her to Scarborough, a place she knew and loved. But although she survived the journey, Anne died a few days after their arrival, slipping away as quietly and unobtrusively as she had lived. To spare her father the pain of yet another funeral, Charlotte arranged for her to be buried in Scarborough.

With two sisters and a brother dead in the same year,

Charlotte faced an agony of loneliness. Ellen Nussey and William Smith Williams did their best to comfort her, but no one could take the place of Emily and Anne. All that she had left was her work, and she turned to it now, deciding to complete a novel which she had started some months earlier. By August it was finished and entitled *Shirley*, but Charlotte herself could not judge its worth. "I shall be curious to hear your opinion," she wrote to Mr. Williams, "my own is of no value."

Shirley, published in October, 1849, is not a second *Jane Eyre*. It contains too much history, too much moralizing, too little feeling and drama. But it was, at the time, a huge success. Her fame increasing, Charlotte began to lead a more social life. There were fairly frequent excursions to London which, though a nervous strain, were interesting and exhilarating. She met Thackeray, her idol; Charles Dickens; Mrs. Trollope; and her future biographer, Mrs. Gaskell.

However, she was still happiest at Haworth, where the arrival of the mailman was henceforth the most exciting hour in her day. Her fame as a writer brought her letters from other writers, and from her many admirers, and she was especially supported by her correspondence with Mr. Williams.

She still felt that she was fated to be a spinster, a notion that was probably encouraged by her father. Mr. Brontë, ailing himself and always concerned about Charlotte's health, found the least allusion to possible matrimony "most offensive." When Charlotte suspected that Mr. Nicholls, the Haworth curate, was beginning to be interested in her, she did not encourage him, although she must have longed for sympathetic companionship.

A visitor to Haworth at that time described the parsonage in telling terms. "A dreary, dreary place literally paved with rain-blackened tombstones. . . . There was the house before us, a small oblong stone house, with not a tree to screen it from the cutting wind. Miss Brontë put me so much in mind of her own Jane Eyre. . . . There is something touching in the sight of that little creature entombed in such a place, and moving about herself like a spirit."

There were interruptions to the loneliness. Charlotte made a new friend in Harriet Martineau whom she visited at her home in the Lake District. She paid brief visits to London, where James Taylor, her publisher's reader and editor, paid her attentions which seemed to be the prelude to a declaration. There was a visit to Mrs. Gaskell and her children.

And of course there was her writing, this time her master-piece, *Villette*. Published in January, 1853, it was largely autobiographical, Villette, of course, being Brussels. The doubts and agonies of her feeling for M. Héger are here translated into a dramatic and moving love story, in which imagination and reality are sensitively interwoven. "There is more of Charlotte herself in *Villette* than in any of her books," says Margaret Crompton, one of her biographers. "In Lucy Snowe's history we can trace her own creed of fatalistic distrust: 'The negation of severe suffering was the nearest approach to happiness I expected to know.' "

In December, 1852, Mr. Nicholls, the curate, suddenly proposed marriage to Charlotte. "He spoke of sufferings he had borne for months," she wrote to Ellen Nussey, "of suffer-ings he could endure no longer, and craved leave for some hope. I could only entreat him to leave me then and promise a reply on the morrow."

Hearing of the offer, Mr. Brontë, then seventy-five, was so infuriated that Charlotte refused Mr. Nicholls on the follow-ing day. A little later he left Haworth, and Charlotte, deeply sympathetic with his suffering on her behalf, began a correspondence with him. His absence depressed her, and even visits from such friends as Mrs. Gaskell did nothing to lift her spirits.

After her suitor had paid two clandestine visits to Haworth, Charlotte managed to convince her father that marriage to Mr. Nicholls would benefit Mr. Brontë as well as make Charlotte herself happy. Mr. Nicholls could run the parish, and the trio could live comfortably on their combined incomes. Sensing that his daughter had made up her mind, Mr. Brontë gave in, and Charlotte, "looking like a snowdrop," was married on June 29, 1854.

"Wanted continually . . . constantly called for and occupied," Charlotte was well content with married life. Arthur Nicholls' extreme possessiveness pleased rather than upset her. As a writer, however, she would probably have been seriously hindered had she lived; she told Ellen Nussey that her duties as a clergyman's wife left her no leisure for writing.

The end to her brief period of happiness came with shocking speed. Catching cold after a winter walk on the moors, she took to her bed with continuous attacks of sickness and faintness. The collapse of Tabby, their faithful old servant, at eighty-four, grieved her sadly; so did the death of Anne's little dog, Flossy. Doctors, summoned to examine her, felt that her congenial but demanding life as a married woman had put the final strain on her delicate constitution. There was nothing they could do for her.

In March she had frequent periods of delirium and began to sink. Her husband, numb with grief, watched over her tenderly, and it was he to whom her thoughts turned at the last. "Oh, I am not going to die, am I?" she asked. "He will not separate us. We have been so happy."

On March 31, 1855, she died, her husband and her father at her bedside. "Perhaps it was an ideal moment to die," says

Margaret Crompton in *Passionate Search*. "She was completely happy, surrounded by love and tenderness, and with no qualms about a future which might have brought disillusion."

GEORGE ELIOT

[1819–1880]

O<small>NE OF THE</small> most powerful women thinkers of the nineteenth century, George Eliot was born on November 22,
1819, during a period of transition in English history. The last
of the great Napoleonic wars had been fought. The era of
world-shaking inventions had not yet begun. The land was at
rest, undisturbed by the shriek of the railroad whistle. War-
wickshire, the author's birthplace, was a county of pasture-
land, meadows, and slow brown canals. Everything in her
environment encouraged George Eliot's tendency to reflection and introspection.

She was born Mary Ann Evans, younger daughter of
Robert Evans, a land agent *"unique* among land agents for his
manifold knowledge and experience." A man of great physical strength, with a prodigious memory which his daughter
inherited from him, he was a tireless worker, conscientious
and methodical. Marian, as she was soon called by everyone,
gave him unquestioning admiration; as a child, she often
accompanied him on his rounds, drinking in his views on
government as the gig bowled along the country lanes. Later
she was to immortalize him in the lovable characters of Adam
Bede and Caleb Garth.

Her mother, Christiana Pearson, was a voluble, home-loving

woman who appeared in *Adam Bede* as the earthy and commonsensible Mrs. Poyser. Marian, the ugly duckling of the family, was less to her mother's taste than was her sister Chrissy, a neat and pretty child. When, early in her schooldays, Marian showed evidence of an exceptional mind, Mrs. Evans was dubious rather than pleased. In their younger daughter, she suspected, "they had a sport for which the family history on either side would hardly account."

Marian's childhood is vividly described in the autobiographical parts of her novels. In *The Mill on the Floss*, Tom Tulliver is patterned on her brother Isaac, whom she tagged after adoringly, and imitated to the best of her ability. She, herself, in everything but physical appearance, was the model for Maggie.

Like the Tullivers, Isaac and Marian made their own amusements. They climbed about in the barns and haylofts of their farm home, Griff House. They chased each other through the tall meadow grass, scrambled down the disused quarry, and searched for traces of gypsy encampments. Together they stood staring at the slow-moving barges, while Marian "pondered endlessly the mystery of the land into which that strange cargo of coal and men and tattered children and little smoking chimney was floating."

During her school years, first at Nuneaton and later at Coventry, Marian turned from a boisterous tomboy into something of a prig. With her burning need to love and admire, she modeled herself so closely on two of her teachers, Maria Lewis and Rebecca Franklin, that her own personality went into eclipse. A young paragon, she organized clothing clubs, visited the poor, and was the first to speak up during prayer meetings. When she returned to Griff House for the holidays, she did her best to convert the pleasure-loving Isaac to more godly ways. Loving his comforts and pastimes, Isaac resisted stoutly.

During her adolescence, cruel demands were made of Marian and her sister. Little more than children, they had to nurse their hopelessly ill mother until her death. Their father recovered from a serious illness but never regained his strength and vigor. Chrissy escaped the desolate home through marriage, but Marian, refusing her father's offer to engage a housekeeper, took it upon herself to run the household.

Although she relished the importance of her position and the authority it gave her, she was unhappy in the years that followed. True, her days were full and fruitful; she studied languages with visiting tutors, continued her good works, read omnivorously, and wrote long, analytical letters to her former teachers. But these activities failed to satisfy her. A thinker, she had no one with whom to share her thoughts. Craving love, she had no young friend to cherish and be cherished by.

Neither her work nor her religion were of real comfort at this time. Although she read widely, she made no attempt to write anything of her own. Instead, she began a formidable project, the compiling of an Ecclesiastical Chart. "It gives a chronological view of Ecclesiastical History," she wrote to a friend, "and has not that I know of been forestalled." She was wrong; before she could finish this arid task, a rival chart appeared. Marian abandoned her own forthwith, without regret but with the frustrating knowledge that she now had no outlet through which to pass on her fund of accumulated learning to others.

There was little gaiety in her temperament. Her religion was too repressive. When the Franklins took her to a concert, she could not permit herself to enjoy it and wrote to Maria Lewis, "It would not cost me any regrets if the only music heard in our land were that of strict worship."

Isaac's engagement, and the news that her father meant to turn Griff House over to him and his bride, deepened her depression. When, in 1840, she and Robert Evans moved to Bird Grove, Coventry, the future looked bleak and empty. She did not suspect that a new and exhilarating phase of her life was about to begin.

Congenial companionship was waiting for her. The Franklin sisters, Mary and Rebecca, lived within walking distance. Mrs. Sibree, a minister's wife, came calling. She brought with her Mary, her sixteen-year-old daughter, and her son, John. Although they were at first repelled by Marian's ugliness, the youngsters were soon worshiping at the shrine of her intellect. Best of all, Marian was introduced to Charles Bray and his wife Caroline, and for the first time reveled in a friendship that was warm and spontaneous as well as intellectual.

At the outset it was Charles, rather than his wife, who captured her interest. He had turned his back on revealed religion and had formulated his own beliefs in a statement which he published as *Inquiry*. This was followed by his masterpiece, *The Philosophy of Necessity*, after which he and his wife gave up church-going altogether.

The Brays found a potential disciple in the impressionable Marian. "We soon found that her mind was already turned towards greater freedom of thought in religious expression," Charles said. Husband and wife welcomed her to their inner circle, pressed books upon her, and involved her in discussions on "subjects under heaven and on earth." Soon Marian was questioning her own beliefs—and deciding that she was living a lie.

When, in her uncompromising way, she broke it to her father that she would no longer attend church with him, Robert Evans was aghast—and furious. Hoping to bring her to her senses, he threatened to give up Bird Grove and go and live with Chrissy. But he allowed Marian a little time and sent her to Isaac to think things over. Griff House, with its tender memories of her childhood, reminded her of her years of attachment to her father; Marian decided that she could at least give him the shadow of conformity. Her mind would remain free. Within a month, she returned home, to accompany her father to church—but to spend as much time as possible with the Brays.

At Rosehill, the Bray home, she met many freethinkers. One was Sara Hennell, Caroline's sister, like Marian an ardent seeker after truth. Another was Rufa Brabant, a scholarly young woman who was engaged to Sara's brother, Charles.

When Rufa married, she gave up the work she was engaged on, a translation of Strauss' *Das Leben Jesu*. At the urging of the Brays, Marian took over the task, a grueling undertaking which occupied her for two and a quarter years. Then, ready for diversion, she went to visit Sara in Clapham, London. Caroline was coaxed to join them. "Please come in a very mischievous, unconscientious, theatre-loving humour," Marian wrote gaily.

The death of her father ended the second phase of Marian's experience, leaving her sunk in depression and fearful of the future. Her melancholy persisted, even when the Brays took her to Europe and showed her the beauties and antiquities of Paris, the Riviera, the Italian Lakes, and Switzerland. When they left for England, Marian stayed on in Geneva. "I will never go near a friend again until I can bring joy and peace in my heart and in my face," she declared.

Settling down as a paying guest of the D'Albert family, Marian was agreeably entertained. François D'Albert was Conservateur of the town's art gallery, an artist, a musician, and an excellent conversationalist. His wife, Marian wrote home, was "a really ladylike person, who says everything well." She had no wish to leave Geneva. "I can only think with a shudder of returning to England," she said. "It looks to me like a land of gloom, of *ennui*, of platitude."

But after a social winter she became homesick for her English friends. She returned temporarily to Rosehill, sure of only one thing—that she wanted to earn her living by writing reviews for scholarly journals.

Her opportunity came when Chapman, the publisher of her translation of *Das Leben Jesu*, invited her to become assistant editor of the *Westminster Review*, which he had just acquired. Moving to London, Marian soon found herself in the center of a circle consisting of some of the most advanced thinkers and brilliant writers of the day, among them Harriet Martineau, novelist and economist, and the philosopher Herbert Spencer, whose writings influenced contemporary philosophy, psychology, and ethics throughout Europe and America, India and Japan.

Marian plunged eagerly into the work at hand; she chose contributors for the *Review*, wrote and edited articles, and produced lengthy reviews in French and German. Life was more satisfying than it had ever been—she had faithful old friends; new ones like Barbara Leigh Smith, "the incarnation of radiant health and unconventionalism"; and an assured position in the intellectual world of London. Besides working hard for the *Review*, she read intensively, concentrating on the work of women writers and unconsciously preparing herself for her later career.

The third phase of her life dates from the beginning of her acquaintance with George Henry Lewes, literary and dramatic critic and author of *Life of Goethe* and *A Biographical History of Philosophy*. An ugly but highly pleasant little man, Lewes had married a beauty by whom he had two sons before she forsook him for another man. He sought Marian out not only because he admired her work but because he felt that she would give him sympathy and understanding. Marian found this appeal irresistible; "for the first time she was asked to support, instead of hoping she might lean."

Marian and Lewes formed a close and enduring friendship, each remaining devoted to the other's aims and interests. It was Lewes, in his abiding respect for her genius, who was responsible for Marian's birth as a novelist. One day, as they walked together, he wondered aloud whether her greatest gift might not be for fiction. "You must try to write a story," he told her. She considered—and agreed. Soon she was writing, and underlining, in her diary, "I am anxious to begin my fiction writing."

Within two weeks she completed a short story, "Amos Barton." Lewes submitted it to *Blackwood's Magazine*, without revealing its authorship. The story was accepted and Marian, encouraged, wrote two more, "Mr. Gilfil's Love Story" and "Janet's Repentance." In 1858 these were collected as *Scenes from Clerical Life;* a new departure in English literature, they "represented the clergy like every other class with the humours, sorrows and troubles of other men." Marian began to sign herself "George Eliot," George after Lewes, and Eliot because it was "a good mouth-filling, easily pronounced word."

The book was enthusiastically received, especially by Charles Dickens, the only reader perceptive enough to guess the sex of its author. Confident now, Marian embarked on her first novel. She meant it to be "a country story, full of the breath of cows and the scent of hay," and decided that it should include some recollections of her father. A resounding success, *Adam Bede* was the first realistic pastoral novel, a presentation of the English country scene which put her in the front rank of contemporary novelists.

Its success had gratifying results. It enabled Marian to purchase her first home, the large but unprepossessing Holly Lodge. It brought letters and visits from such notables as Wilkie Collins, Bulwer-Lytton, Mrs. Gaskell, and Charles Dickens. Content and happy, she left for the tour of Italy which she had long promised herself.

Three years passed before Marian started a new novel, although she had been nursing the idea for five years. The book grew slowly, "like a sickly child." Marian, never in good health, was morbidly afraid that her writing had deteriorated after *Adam Bede,* and Lewes, her chief support, was ailing and unable to give her his usual cheer and comfort. To some extent, her premonitions were right. *Felix Holt* was not wholly successful, although its author wrote of the people and places she knew best. Its story was melodramatic, and its leading character was so idealized as to seem incredible. But Blackwood, her publisher, was well satisfied; he even declared the book to be superior to *Adam Bede.*

The next year was a tranquil one. Independent of money worries, Marian could please herself about what she wrote, and she did so by composing a verse drama, *The Spanish Gypsy.* That finished, she took frequent trips abroad and, when at home, enjoyed the companionship of Lewes and did much entertaining in her second home, The Priory. But Lewes' health worsened, and both he and Marian suffered a tragedy in the death of his beloved son Thornton.

For a time, Marian busied herself with shorter compositions, including a long short story, "Miss Brooke." To her surprise, she found that she was writing better than ever. Deeply attracted to the character of Miss Brooke, she incorporated the story into her next novel, *Middlemarch,* a very long book which was published in eight monthly parts.

Middlemarch was immediately acclaimed, and rightly so. It

has its faults; there are exaggerations and idealizations which make some of the characters unreal. "But *Middlemarch*," say her biographers, Lawrence and Elizabeth Hanson, "stands out as the mature product of a deeply feeling, deeply thinking mind whose like has not been seen again. In it, a section of English life hitherto unregarded and unchronicled is opened up with a comprehensiveness and skill that . . . remain wholly admirable and, in their own sphere, unsurpassed."

The next four years were a time of comfort, happiness, and financial success, although marred by Marian's persistent minor ailments and by her concern for Lewes' health. She wrote nothing at the time, but was mulling over an idea for her next novel. In it, she intended to advocate a cause with which she was deeply sympathetic—the establishment of a Jewish state. *Daniel Deronda*, the first part of which appeared in February, 1876, was inspired by her own and Lewes' admiration for Emmanel Deutsch, "a very dear, delightful creature" who was the leader of a "Back to Palestine" movement. Although it is overburdened with propaganda and is too experimental and realistic, the book has much of interest and in certain parts is as good as anything she ever wrote.

Marian was by now a social as well as literary success, received even by royalty. She and Lewes broadened their already large circle of friends, and Marian achieved another ambition when she purchased a handsome house with magnificent views of the Surrey hills called The Heights. Here, and in her "warmer nest in town," she entertained frequently, with Lewes trying bravely to ignore his ill health. Both made a new friend in John Cross, a younger man who greatly admired Marian's work and personality.

In October, 1878, Marian took what was to be her last journey. She and Lewes paid a visit to Cross' brother-in-law in Newmarket, where their fellow guests were Oscar Browning and Turgenev, the Russian novelist. Soon after they returned, Lewes fell ill, but he recovered sufficiently to send Marian's newly completed essays, *Impressions of Theophrastus Such*, to her publisher. A few days later he became "alarmingly ill," and on November 28, he died.

Marian was inconsolable. She wrote no letters and saw no one except Lewes' son Charles until the New Year. Then, slowly, she began to recover. "She had lived over this loss many times before it happened," said her biographers. "The reality, shattering though it was, had therefore been forestalled and stripped of its worst terrors." She was helped to some degree by the attentions of John Cross, who persistently sought her out. He, too, craved consolation after the death of his mother.

During the year 1879, Cross was her constant companion. He took her out frequently—to the National Gallery, the museums of South Kensington, and to see the drawings at the Grosvenor Gallery and the Old Masters at the Academy. By March of the following year, exulting that she now felt alive again, she agreed to marry him.

She had no inkling that her own life was soon to end, and was anticipating a full and harmonious union when they settled into Cross' house in Cheyne Walk, London. Together, they arranged her thousands of books. They began to entertain their friends, keeping open house on Sundays. Every evening, Marian played the piano for her husband.

In December she caught cold—a cold which attacked her heart. "There was no strength in her to resist it," Cross told her friends. "From the time the doctor examined her, she became completely unconscious and passed away at 10 o'clock without any apparent struggle or pain." The date was December 22, 1880.

Returning to Lewes in death, she was buried beside him, in Highgate Cemetery, London.

MARY WEBB

[1881-1927]

$\mathcal{A}$ superb novelist of country life, Mary Webb had a long wait for recognition, even after Rebecca West pronounced her "a genius," and England's prime minister, Stanley Baldwin, himself a Shropshire man, wrote delightedly about her *Precious Bane:* "In your book I seem to hear again the speech and turns of phrase which surrounded me in the nursery. I think it is a really first-class piece of work. . . . Thank you a thousand times for it."

Perhaps her use of the Shropshire dialect makes Mary Webb's books a little difficult, although few readers will have trouble in getting Prue Sarn's meaning when she says things like, "I pulled all the white roses and a tuthree pinks that were in blow. . . ." More probably the reader needs to be something of a mystic if he is to grasp the full beauty and significance of her work.

Mary Webb was born Gladys Mary Meredith, in the Shropshire village of Leighton-under-the-Wrekin on March 25, 1881. Except for schooling in Southport, Lancashire, and brief sojourns in Chester and London, she spent her whole life in that county and felt herself an exile when she crossed its border. Shropshire's poet laureate, A. E. Housman, shared her inexhaustible pleasure in its countryside and his *A Shropshire*

Lad had a lasting influence on her development.

Her father, George Edward Meredith, was a man of great charm, kindly, unselfish, humble. His grandfather and father had been, in turn, Vicar of Leighton Parish Church, but he himself earned a living coaching pupils for the universities and for Sandhurst, England's Royal Military College. An outdoor man, he gardened, sketched, painted and—to his daughter's chagrin—kept greyhounds and a pack of beagles. Mary Webb recalls him fondly in her poem, "Treasures."

> These are my treasures: just a word, a look,
> A chiming sentence from his favorite book,
> A large, blue scented blossom that he found
> And picked for me in some enchanted ground,
> A joy he planned for us, a verse he made
> Upon a birthday. . . .

From her father, Mary inherited not only her love of the countryside but her amused, yet kindly, interest in such rustic figures as the cowman, "Owd Blossom." In her story of the same name, she tells us how, on Sunday afternoons, "he would lean over a gate, or lie on the hillside, and brood upon the plain. Nothing ever came of his broodings, at least there was never anything that anyone could see. He would shake back his flaxen hair, chew a stalk of bracken, and murmur 'I like a sunset.' That was all."

Her mother, Sarah Alice Meredith, was the daughter of an Edinburgh physician, a domesticated woman with lovable idiosyncracies. She claimed kinship with Sir Walter Scott, although on the flimsiest evidence. Her daughter, in a Christmas poem, remembers her mother's way of guarding her most cherished possessions in her room.

> Within the doorway of your room tonight
> I stood, and saw your little treasures all
> Set out beneath the golden candle light.

In 1882, when Mary was a year old, the Merediths moved to the old Shropshire town of Much Wenlock, where they lived for the next fourteen years. Her first six years set a pattern of joy in solitude. After that, five brothers and sisters were born, all within seven years.

Theirs was a happy, sheltered life. There were prayers and Bible-reading in the family circle, and devotional books on the shelf, but their piety was not restrictive, and if the young Mary really worshiped anything, it was Nature. Less robust than her brothers and sisters, she seldom took part in their games, preferring to roam the lanes and meadows, savoring her delight in trees, birds, and flowers. "As a child," she said later, "I remember standing awe-stricken at the strange beauty of a well-known field in the magic of a June dawn."

Much Wenlock had its comical aspects for her. She called it "a very Rip Van Winkle of a borough." The old beadle who, during Sunday service, rapped fidgety boys on the head with his stick "until you would think a woodpecker had come to church" roused her mirth—but it was she who read the Bible to him once a week, never forgetting his favorite passage.

During the years in Much Wenlock, the young Mary—Glad, as everyone called her—made a friend of Miss E. M. Lory, who helped her with her studies and prepared her for the school in Southport to which she was sent when she was fourteen, Miss Lory did more for her development than did the alien "finishing school." She read Shakespeare to her by the hour, fostering Mary's lifelong love of Shakespearean poetry and drama.

When Mary was sixteen, the family moved again, this time to Stanton-on-Hine Heath, where they lived in The Woodlands, described by Thomas Moult, one of Mary's biographers, as a "blossom-fragrant, bird-haunted house." It was difficult to keep the young girl indoors; she even ate many of

her meals in solitude on the lawn. She roamed the countryside, alone or with her father, minutely examining the leaves
and flowers, studying the habits of the birds and talking with
village characters whom she later introduced into her novels.

But in spite of her outdoor life she was a frail girl,
threatened by the pernicious anemia which caused her early
death. The task given to her by her mother, that of supervis-
ing the studies of the younger children, was too great a strain.
Shortly before their next move, this time to Meole Brace, a
village two miles south of Shrewsbury, her health broke
down completely. During her long convalescence, consoled
and inspired by the view from her window, she began to
write essays and poems.

By this time she had outgrown the religion of her childhood and was reading Darwin and Haeckel. "The result of all
this proved to be a pagan one," her brother said later. "Her
God was Nature." So intensely did she respond to natural
beauty that she could never forget the horror she had felt
when her parents decided to cut down the high hawthorn
hedge at their home in Meole Brace. Her emotion is captured
in "To the World," one of the poems included in her collected poetry.

> You took the rare blue from my cloudy sky;
> You shot the one bird in my silent wood;
> You crushed my rose—one rose alone had I.
> You have not known. You have not understood.

Mary Webb's poems, which were not published in book
form until after her death, are in the main descriptive or
meditative. One of her most touching, "An Old Woman,"
voices a deeply felt belief; that we should remember our
neighbor in life rather than in death. The poem ends:

> If there had come, to cheer her loneliness,
> But one red rose, in youth's rose-loving day,

A smile, a tear,
It had been good. But now she goes her way
And does not hear.

Keenly alive to the sufferings of humanity, Mary Webb
had her own sorrow to bear when her father died in 1911.
Her grief brought a return of her illness, and invalidism did
not suit her. "She was so active, mentally and physically," said
one of her neighbors, "that she got no proper rest when she
was ill."

In 1912, she married Henry Bertram Law Webb, a Shrewsbury schoolmaster. Compatible in every way, they were
happy together for fifteen years. When, shortly after their
marriage, Henry took a position in the elegant resort of
Weston-super-Mare, they both hungered for their native
Shropshire. "We were two people who felt at home in old
clothes," he explained, "corduroys, or, in Mary's case, a faded
sunbonnet. The people of Weston-super-Mare would have
felt far from at home in them."

During this period Mary made tentative notes for a novel,
The Golden Arrow. Essays and poems had become too con-
fining; she needed a medium through which she could write
of life as a whole. When they left Weston-super-Mare for
their first real home, Rose Cottage in Pontesbury, she began
to write with amazing speed, finishing *The Golden Arrow* in
three weeks. Its theme was love, and the disillusion which
follows when man and wife do not love each other in the
same way or to the same degree.

In 1914, the outbreak of war and the vision of "a world so
black with hate" spelled agony for Mary's sensitive spirit. Her
three brothers went overseas, where one of them, Mervyn,
was soon seriously wounded. Henry Webb's health suffered
and Mary, always quixotically generous, could not make their
small income stretch to cover both their living expenses and
her charities.

Characteristically, she turned to nature for strength and comfort. With a need to feel herself close to the earth again, she decided to sell the fruit and flowers which they grew in their garden. Day after day, she trudged the nine miles to her market stall in Shrewsbury. She made only a few shillings, but her husband tells us that "she came back looking much brighter: she felt she had done something beautiful."

This experience, unconventional in that time and place but nonetheless wholly satisfying, ended when they moved to The Nills, a farmhouse which they had to leave temporarily when Henry was offered an excellent position in a school in Cheshire. They were soon obliged to spend their week ends at The Nills; it was the only place where Mary could write. Here she completed her second novel, *Gone to Earth*, the story of Hazel, a child of nature, innocent and pitiful, who is crushed by the evil force of materialism.

In 1916, by what seemed a miracle, the Webbs contrived to buy "a field, delightfully untamed," in Lyth. They built a simple, one-story house, with a view of cornfields and misty hills. Mary settled happily to her third novel, *The House in Dormer Forest*, the story of a long-neglected manor and its sinister influence on the family who lived in it.

By the end of World War I, Mary Webb had had three novels accepted by appreciative publishers, but the general public remained indifferent. With her fourth novel, her spirit flagged; *Seven for a Secret* falls below the level of her other work. Her doctor prescribed a change and the Webbs moved to London, where Henry found a teaching position. But the prescription was not a success. Mary hated the city and gave vent to her feelings in her poem, "Freedom":

> . . . Let us away, out of the murky day
> Of sullen towns, into the silver noise
> Of woods where every bird has found her way
> Sunward, and every leaf has found a voice.

After a lonely stay in their house in Lyth, she decided on a compromise. The Webbs found a tucked-away cottage in the old part of London's Hampstead. Here, although she would never be content in any city, Mary had new and happy experiences. She wrote reviews and short stories for the *English Review*, joined the world-famous P.E.N. Club— and met a kindred spirit in the poet, Walter de la Mare.

But she was in poor health, depressed by the public neglect of her work, and chronically short of money. "Mary's earlier sympathy for the poor and suffering had steadily grown into a veritable passion for giving," says Hilda Addison, who wrote a critique of Mary Webb's work. "She gave extravagantly, with an abandonment which sometimes left her own real necessities unsupplied."

Precious Bane, her fifth novel, took two years to finish; during the writing, she divided her time between Lyth and London. Highly subjective, its story is told by Prudence Sarn, a girl whose facial blemish, a hare lip, is symbolic of Mary Webb's own ill health. Magnificently poetic and imaginative, studded throughout with passages of sheer lyric beauty, it deals with Mary Webb's favorite theme—the clash between spirituality and the forces of materialism.

Although it is her masterpiece, and now famous, *Precious Bane* met with few and feeble reviews at the time of its publication. Mary Webb was disheartened, but scarcely surprised. She had already expressed her contempt for the state of contemporary fiction: "Today the craft of letters has been turned into a strictly commercial transaction, and books are manufactured with the prompt neat aplomb of a pot of factory jam."

Eighteen months after the publication of *Precious Bane*, her spirits soared briefly when the book was "discovered" by the prime minister, Stanley Baldwin. Moved and grateful, she answered his letter warmly and, characteristically, dispatched a little bunch of violets for his writing table.

Precious Bane was to be Mary Webb's last complete book. Although she put two years into her next work, *Armor Wherein He Trusted*, it remains a beautiful fragment. Once more the theme is the conflict between flesh and spirit, but this time the author forsakes Shropshire and sets her story in the Welsh Marshes just after the Norman Conquest.

In the autumn of 1927, Mary Webb returned from a stay in Shropshire so ill and so discouraged that her husband and friends were alarmed. At their urging, she agreed to a complete change of scene and set off, alone, to visit her friend Miss Lory in St. Leonard's-on-Sea.

She never reached Miss Lory's house. When her friend met her at the station, she was aghast at her pallor and exhaustion and took her at once to a nursing home.

Mary Webb's last days were peaceful and happy. Her room had a view of the sea and her friends kept it filled with the flowers she loved. Her husband and brother came to be with her. Thomas Moult, most understanding of biographers, gives a moving picture of her last moments on October 8, 1927: ". . . when Miss Lory arrived at the bedside and placed a bunch of violets in her hand and told her that they would all have tea together in the afternoon, she smiled faintly, and managed to whisper: 'That will be nice.' Those were the last words she uttered; softly she fell into sleep—the hour was noon—and by two o'clock she had passed away without waking."

National Portrait Gallery, London

Fanny Burney

The Brontë Sisters, by their broth

Jane Austen, by her sister Cassandra

George Eliot

Virginia Woolf

Mary Webb

Angus McBean, London

Agatha Christie

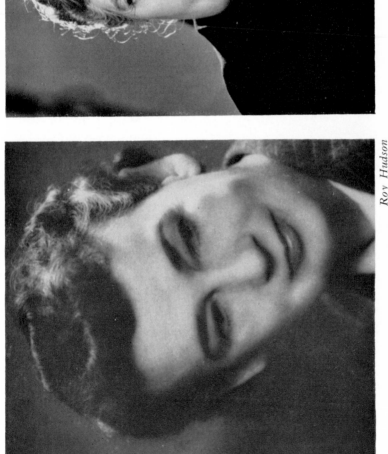

Roy Hudson

Sheila Kaye-Smith

Victoria Sackville-West

Howard Coster

Dorothy L. Sayers

Rumer Godden

Mary Stewart

Studio Lisa Ltd.

VIRGINIA WOOLF

[1882–1941]

ALTHOUGH SHE is also a critic, essayist, and biographer, the rare talents of Virginia Woolf are best revealed in her strange and beautiful novels. Into these she put her whole self, a self dedicated to writing. "She liked writing," says E. M. Forster. "These words, which usually mean so little, must be applied to her with all possible intensity."

One of four children, she was born in London on January 25, 1882, into an upper middle class family which was Victorian in its conventions and way of life. Her mother was Lady Julia Duckworth. Her father, Leslie Stephen, later Sir Leslie, was a distinguished editor and biographer, friend of many of the intellectual leaders of the day.

An agnostic, Stephen gave his children no religious training but passed on to them his deep awareness of the value of human relationships and personal liberty. "He expected certain standards of behaviour, even of ceremony in family life," his daughter tells us. "Yet if freedom means the right to think one's own thoughts and to follow one's own pursuits, then no one respected and indeed insisted on freedom more than he did." Viriginia chose to write, and was allowed the run of her father's library from the time she was fifteen.

After their mother's death when Virginia was thirteen and

her sister Vanessa sixteen, the girls were occasionally tutored by their father. He found the task distasteful, preferring to recite poetry to them or read contemporary novels and the works of Sir Walter Scott. Usually he left them to their own devices while he worked in his study. "As (he) wrote he smoked a short clay pipe, and he scattered books in a circle. The thud of a book dropped on the floor could be heard in the room beneath," Virginia wrote later.

From 1902 onward, ill health made Leslie Stephen dependent on his daughters. He took it for granted that they should stay at home to run his household. Virginia, resentful at finding their leisure curtailed and their freedom of movement restricted, later gave vent to her feelings in *The Angel in the House*. She believed that "the educated man's daughter" should be as free as her brothers to come and go, and felt herself threatened by the nineteenth century convention which kept daughters in subjection. Eventually she rebelled against the role of domestic angel which she was expected to play: "It was she (The Angel in the House) who bothered me and wasted my time and so tormented me that at last I killed her. She was intensely sympathetic. She was immensely charming. She was utterly unselfish. She excelled in the difficult arts of family life. She sacrificed herself daily." The seed of Virginia's feminism, which later flowered in *A Room of One's Own* and *Three Guineas*, was planted at that time.

Release came with the death of Leslie Stephen in 1904. Financially independent, Virginia and Vanessa joined their brothers, Thoby and Adrian, at forty-seven Gordon Square, in Bloomsbury. Thoby brought his Cambridge University friends to call on his sisters, who were quick to appreciate such gifted young men as Clive Bell, Lytton Strachey, and Desmond Macarthy.

Their happiness was short lived. In 1906, while the brothers and sisters were vacationing in Greece, Virginia's beloved Thoby died of typhoid fever. Clive Bell did his best to comfort them in their grief and, within a few months, married Vanessa.

Virginia and Adrian then moved to twenty-nine Fitzroy Square, where the Bells often visited them. Here began the circle of young, talented intellectuals—primarily interested in art and letters, yet aware of the social and political problems of the day—which was later to be known as the Bloomsbury Group. Duncan Grant, a neighbor and friend of the Stephens, described the easy informality of the gatherings in Adrian's study: "About ten in the evening people used to appear, and continue to come at intervals till twelve o'clock at night, and it was seldom that the last guest left before two or three in the morning. Whiskey, cocoa and buns were the diet, and people talked to each other. . . . Conversation, that was all."

Intensely shy, Virginia listened rather than talked, but the milieu suited her to perfection. She was with her equals, young men and women of similar background, with common interests and with the wit to make conversation an art. The Bloomsbury Group respected the reticent young woman, encouraging her and giving her confidence in herself.

In 1912, she married Leonard Woolf, who had recently returned from seven years of administrative work in Ceylon. A student of history, and a confirmed Socialist, he was deeply concerned with social welfare in England, colonial government, and the establishment of the League of Nations.

They were a devoted, wholly congenial couple. Virginia's development owed much to her husband. He shared her love of literature, respected her writing, and broadened her field of interest to include a wider range of people than she had met during her sheltered girlhood. From a shy introvert, she became in time "the center . . . of the literary life of London," says T. S. Eliot. What was of great importance, Leonard Woolf watched over Virginia's health, helping her to ward off the attacks of mental illness which threatened her when her vision of life's darker side became unbearable.

A member of the Bloomsbury Group himself, Woolf recognized it as the ideal testing ground for his wife's talents. The group had its passionate preoccupations with art and beauty, but it also had balance; its members were sensitively concerned with contemporary problems, social and political.

Young, strong, confident, the Group "felt that the world was about to experience a new renaissance, and, what is more, that they were to be leaders in the reawakening." They were soon disillusioned. World War I broke out, threatening life, art, even civilization iteslf. The Group was disrupted, many of its members leaving to enlist or to work for peace. Duncan Grant, Vanessa Bell, Lytton Strachey, and Virginia Woolf now had to write and paint without its stimulation and its sheltering warmth.

Virginia's first novel, *The Voyage Out*, a tragic tale of English tourists in an incredible South American hotel, had been started in the early years of Bloomsbury and was seven years in the writing. It was published in 1915 and followed four years later by *Night and Day*. Both books are strongly subjective; the author, seeking to understand herself and her life, examines her own experiences. The leading characters of *The Voyage Out*, Rachel Vinrace and Terence Hewet, represent the two different sides of Virginia's own character, the dreamy, sensitive, intuitive side and the active, intellectual one. In *Night and Day*, the two sides merge in the character of Katharine Hilbery, like Virginia a divided and contradictory woman.

In 1917, the Woolfs bought a hand printing press, set it up in their home, and founded the Hogarth Press. Its first publication was *Two Stories*, "The Mark on the Wall," by Virginia Woolf, and "Three Jews," by Leonard Woolf, but it soon developed into a publishing house for first editions by writers with original and progressive ideas.

For Virginia, this was a time of acute awareness. "The war," she said, "has shaken the fabric from top to bottom, alienated us from the past and made us perhaps too vividly conscious of the present. Every day we find ourselves doing, saying or thinking things that would have been impossible to our fathers. . . . We have to depend on our senses and emotions."

Her own senses were abnormally active. Wandering around London, she laid herself open to the impressions of the moment, impressions which she recorded with startling vividness in such essays as *Street Haunting: A London Adventure*. "Let us dally," she says. "Let us dally a little longer, be content still with surfaces only—the glossy brilliance of the motor omnibuses; the carnal splendour of the butchers' shops with their yellow flanks and purple steaks; the blue and red bunches of flowers burning so bravely through the plate glass of the florists' windows."

She was as keenly alive to the "delicious society" of her own body, to the delights of satisfying her appetite, bathing, and resting. In *To the Lighthouse*, a later book, she makes poetry out of the *Boeuf en Daube*, "with its confusion of savoury brown and yellow meats and its bay leaves and wine," which had taken the cook three days to make. Still later, in her biography of Flush, Elizabeth Barrett Browning's dog, she delights in describing his sensations. At one point she captures the riot of emotions that flooded Flush's nerves as he stood for the first time in an invalid's bedroom, in Wimpole Street, and smelled eau de cologne. *Flush*, one critic commented, "is doggie without being silly."

In 1921, Virginia Woolf published *Monday or Tuesday*, a volume of short stories in which she used a highly individual technique. She tried to "record the atoms as they fall upon the mind in the order in which they fall." In "Kew Gardens," for example, she follows little groups of people as they stroll past a flower bed, describing them in detail and recording faithfully everything they say or think. E. M. Forster calls these short stories "lovely little things," but adds that they "seemed to lead nowhere, they were all tiny dots and coloured blobs. . . ."

In *Jacob's Room*, which followed in the next year, she uses the same technique. It is an episodic novel, which presents its characters impressionistically and interrupts its story for leisurely discussions about life and literature. An uneven little book, but one with great style and sensitivity, it gives the reader a foretaste of finer novels to come.

With *Mrs. Dalloway* (1925) and *To the Lighthouse* (1927), Virginia contributed a new kind of "stream of consciousness" technique to the English novel. Narrative gives place to strange weavings of impression and memory as the author zigzags between the present and past moods and recollections of her characters. In *To the Lighthouse*, where the heroine looks back upon her life, ten years are contracted into the space of a single day.

Orlando (1928) strikes a completely different note. An understandable book, written with ease and delight, it is the biography of a remarkable character, who is a man in the first half of the book and a woman in the second. Based on the personality of her friend, Victoria Sackville-West, it embraces all of Virginia's own interests—her love of books, her feminism, her pleasure in literary gossip, her desire for a more honest and open treatment of sex—treating them with wit and humor.

One of her feminist books, the charming *A Room of One's Own*, followed in 1929. Mingling feminism with reverie, it traces the history of female education. But the author scarcely plays fair; ignoring anything that might invalidate her argument, she concludes that no woman can be free to write good books until she has an income of five hundred pounds a year, and a room of her own—with a key.

In 1931, she published her finest novel, *The Waves*. In it, during a day at the seashore, framed by the waves, sun, and sea birds, six characters conduct an uninterrupted conversation. It presents the reader with a record of their experiences from childhood to maturity. "If a work of art is to be judged by its capacity for increasing our awareness of life and of ourselves," says M. K. Johnstone, "then *The Waves* is eminently successful."

Her last novels were not as fine as her earlier ones. In *The Years*, she is too intensely aware of the ugliness and horror that underlie the joy and beauty of life. She cannot escape from her bleak vision of poverty, illness, and death. "How terrible old age is," she makes her heroine, Eleanor, think as she looks at her father, "shearing off all one's faculties, one by one, but leaving something alive in the centre."

Between the Acts, published posthumously, is Virginia Woolf's final tribute to the land she loved. Its theme is a village pageant which presents the entire history of England. "She takes us back . . . and she points us on," says E. M. Forster, "and she shows us through her poetic vagueness something more solid than patriotic history and something better worth dying for."

While she was writing *Between the Acts*, the Battle of Britain was being fought. Under its shattering impact, Virginia's personal tragedy moved closer. She began to suffer from numbing fits of depression. She was troubled by a lack of concentration and began to hear the "voices" that presage mental illness.

On January 1, 1941, she made a prophetic entry in her diary. "What is the phrase I always remember—or forget," she asked. "Look your last on all things lovely." Now, wherever she turned, horror followed on the heels of beauty. "Still frost. Burning white. Burning blue. The elms red. I did not mean to describe, once more, the downs in snow; but it came," she wrote on January 9. And a few days later, after a walk in London, she painted a scene of destruction: "So by Tube to the Temple; and there wandered in the desolate ruins of my old squares; gashed, dismantled; the old red bricks all white powder, something like a builder's yard. Grey dirt and broken windows. Sightseers; all that completeness ravished and demolished."

Crushed by the nerve-racking strain of the bombings, overworked, and undernourished, she feared a complete mental breakdown and felt that she would not survive it. On March 28, 1941, she took her own life, drowning herself in the River Ouse.

The literary world was shocked and grieved. Her husband and close friends, long aware of her overwrought sensibility, had no doubt feared some such tragedy. E. M. Forster, who had known and admired her from the beginning of her writing career, delivered a warning to the sensation monger. "The epitaph of such a writer cannot be written by the vulgar-minded or the lugubrious. Virginia Woolf got through an immense amount of work, she gave acute pleasure in new ways, she pushed the light of the English language a little further against the darkness."

SHEILA KAYE-SMITH

[1887-1956]

ONE OF ENGLAND's most prolific women novelists, Sheila
Kaye-Smith was born in St. Leonard's-on-Sea, in the county
of Sussex, in 1887. She was fortunate in her birthplace for
Sussex is a county rich in historical and literary associations
and in beauty and variety of landscape. It has downs and
woodlands, marshes and meandering streams, orchards and
hop gardens. A happy hunting ground for the archaeologist,
it has a great number of prehistoric camps, earthworks, and
burial mounds. Small wonder that this author set so many of
her novels in Sussex past and present.

Sheila was the eldest child of compatible parents, a wid-
ower and widow who married in middle life. Edward Kaye-
Smith, a physician and surgeon, came of East Anglian stock;
his wife was part French, part Scottish. She took her daughters on many visits to Scotland, and for years Sheila's heart
was "in a frenzy of devotion" not only to the house of Stuart
but to "the blue stencil of the Highland Hills beyond Perth,
the cloud-hung rocks of Glen Affric and Strathmore, the
cliffs of Mam Soul and the little snow-filled corries of the
Cairn Gorms."

A doctor of the old school, "with a doorbell in constant
agitation," Edward Kaye-Smith could afford to keep his

family in considerable comfort. He believed that food should be enjoyed and taught his daughters to be discriminating about it. Much later, during World War II, Sheila Kaye-Smith wrote a book on wartime cookery; it is charmingly discursive because, for her, food "has too many associations in life and memory to be isolated as a subject."

There was no servant problem during her youth. "My mother kept three maids beside our nurse," she tells us. "Indeed, when I was very young there was also a nursemaid. Besides the nursery staff we had a cook, a house parlourmaid, and a housemaid." Later, with amused affection, she recalls Emily, the wasp-killing maid at Platnix Farm where they spent many vacations. "She had bare red arms and a mottled red face and she used to kill 'wopses' with her thumb."

For Sheila, religion was part of everyday life. There was nothing restrictive about it, however, and even the hell-fire sermons she heard in Scotland did not upset her. She saw God as a loving, if remote, Father and was quietly devoted to His Son. Her parents, Low Anglicans, were amused rather than disquieted when she voiced her belief in the Pope as the head of the Church. From childhood, she was attracted by ritual and ceremonies; with her younger sister, Moira, she used to conduct Divine Service for their dolls every Sunday "amid many quarrels as to rite and precedence."

The little girls were brought up sensibly, but with sympathetic indulgence on their mother's part. When the small Sheila started a custom of carrying home from their neighbor's tea party whatever she could not eat on the spot, her mother, says Sheila, "was never more ashamed of me in her life. . . . But she did nothing to stop me."

It was in the home of this neighbor, a kindly spinster named Miss Arabella, that Sheila cultivated her taste for history. Knowing that the small girl despised fairy stories, Miss Arabella would bring out "THE HISTORY BOOKS . . . infinite in number and overwhelming in size. They were certainly not written for children, being very closely printed in a number of dark columns with only a few, quite documentary illustrations. But for me," says Sheila, "they were the perfect escape, the perfect franchise."

Her longest-lived childhood hero was Charles Edward Stuart, the Young Pretender, about whom she wrote countless tales, some of them novel length. While still at school, she wrote thirteen novels, all historical, each averaging 22,000 words. This fluency was probably the reason for two of her few faults as a novelist—her books were sometimes too similar, and she repeated herself too frequently.

She attended school from 1896 to 1904 but was not, like her mother before her, compelled to study such domestic arts as cookery and needlework. Nor, when she left school, was she obliged to fill up her "sacks of leisure" with elaborate social activities, desultory attempts at self-improvement, or experimental "good works." Her writing absorbed her completely, and her first novel was accepted soon after she left school. "I was an author," she wrote later, "a real, professional, paid author, so I did not have to search for occupation. When I was not actually writing, I was walking, cycling or riding in the country—in the fields, lanes and villages where my heart and my work were both set."

During adolescence, her interest in religion had fluctuated. At times, for example when she learned that there were people called atheists who did not believe in God, her own faith wavered. But it was restored on the feast of the Conversion of St. Paul, who, she was certain, "had first-hand information" about the existence of God.

She believed that the problems of religion made excellent material for novels. "Actually," she said in later years, "religion provides nearly as many good situations as the sex instinct—there are endless combinations, permutations, frustrations and deviations which the novelist can use, and its effects on character (whether by its growth or its thwarting) makes something new in the way of psychological interest."

In her first novel, she proved to her own satisfaction and that of her readers that the appearance of religion in a story did not necessarily make for dullness or pious platitudinizing. *The Tramping Methodist*, considered almost a "thriller" in its day, told of the wanderings of an itinerant preacher through the country the young author loved best.

When she was twenty-one, her publishers suggested that she should spend some time in London for the purpose of widening her experience. She went meekly enough; she did not, however, venture beyond her own social sphere, and such independence as she reached showed itself chiefly in her attitude to religion. Taken to visit Alice Meynell, the well-known Catholic poetess, essayist, and mother of novelist Viola Meynell, Sheila was impressed by the atmosphere of ease and culture in the Meynell home but reacted perversely to the family's Catholic faith. Like any young intellectual, she felt she must throw her old beliefs overboard and become liberal and "progressive." She read Nietzche, Swedenborg, and Madame Blavatsky, whose influence was visible in her next novel, *Spell Land*. This novel, which originally had a governess for its heroine, ended up with a Swedenborgian minister for its main character. It was a gripping yarn, in spite of the incongruity of introducing so alien a religion into a tale of the Sussex weald.

The proceeds from *Spell Land* were enough to finance a trip to Paris, one which had to be abruptly curtailed when she contracted pneumonia and had to return to England for a long period of convalescence. During this time, she found herself unhappy without formal religion, so returned to her early beliefs although they did not completely satisfy her. The next twelve years, she tells us, she spent "as a sort of synthetic Catholic in the Church of England." At the end of this time she married Theodore Penrose Fry, an Anglican clergyman with a parish in St. Leonard's-on-Sea.

Because his rector believed in celibacy and would not employ a married curate, the Frys left for Notting Dale, London—but Sheila took the precaution of buying an ancient oast-house, a building that once housed a hop-drying kiln, in Sussex, so that she would always have a home in her beloved county. Later they were transferred to a rather poor parish in South Kensington where Sheila was disturbed by the pomp and magnificence of the church in contrast to its drab surroundings. She was also upset by the continual disputes between Anglo-Catholics and Protestant factions in the Church of England. Before long, she found herself drawn to the strength and stability of the Roman Catholic Church.

Her religious waverings soon came to an end, oddly enough through the medium of her husband. Fry, as a result of the controversies centering around the Revised Prayer Book, had begun to doubt the validity of the Church of England. In admitting his feelings to his wife he found that she, like himself, was being inexplicably drawn to the Catholic Church. Shocked at what they both considered to be a temptation against their faith, they decided that what they were suffering from was an attack of "Roman Fever" and hurried away on a cruise to Sicily, supposedly the infallible cure for anyone with inclinations toward Rome. They expected to see the Catholic Church "at its most repulsive" in Southern Europe and believed that they would return home thanking heaven that they were Anglicans.

But in their case the remedy failed to work. Visiting the

cathedral at Palermo, they could not help comparing it with the Anglican cathedrals in England. The latter, they decided regretfully, were austerely beautiful but cold and museum-like, whereas the cathedral of Palermo was "a cheerful, lively, democratic spiritual home." Leaving Palermo, they felt a pang of loss, a suspicion that they were exchanging a warm and broad faith for one that was cold and limited.

Back in England, her husband gave up his ministry and they both took instructions and were received into the Catholic Church. As might be expected, the author's readers leveled a fire of criticism at her. They waited sceptically for her next novel, certain that from now on she would write only "religious propaganda" and would be ruined as a novelist.

But, far from watering down or dehumanizing her work, the new religious affiliation brought to the novels of Sheila Kaye-Smith a greater depth of substance and new significance. Her next novel, *Susan Spray*, was a dramatic story of the visit to England of a notorious American woman evangelist. *The Ploughman's Progress* dealt with the problems of farm laborers during the slump. Her first two novels of specific Catholic interest, *Superstition Corner* and *Galleybird*, are not only "religious" but social and historical. She based them on a legend that, in times when the Catholic Church was being persecuted in England, Mass was secretly celebrated at Tufton, near her home; one of the local place names, Superstition Corner, belonged most probably to the crossroads near the reputed Mass-house. She intended to give the story of the neighborhood from the banishment of the Mass in 1559 down to the return of the Mass in 1930, at which time it was said in a loft in Little Doucegrove, her own home. Actually, she carried the story no farther than the seventeenth century, but the two books make lively and absorbing reading.

Following them came a change of pace. *The Children's*

Summer and *Selina Is Older*, delightful minglings of fact and fiction, recapture the happiness of her childhood days. In *Three Ways Home*, she wrote her spiritual autobiography, a book of great simplicity and sincerity.

During World War II, the Frys remained at their home in Rye "with the German army about 42 miles away and sending over tokens of its presence at Teutonically regular intervals." During the first phase of the war, Sheila and her husband sheltered a number of refugees from bomb-threatened London, and Sheila was amused, but sympathetic, about their verdicts on the countryside, "of which 'mortuary' and 'cemetery' were the least offensive." She managed to get on well with these city-bred evacuees, many of whom were mothers with young children. "Certainly we all liked one another and when Christmas came parted the best of friends, my mothers having given their rooms a clean-out that included even the windows but excluded for some reason the floors. My regret at their departure," she says, "was regarded in the village as a morbid symptom."

In the second phase of the war, she turned her attention to cooking and took a few lessons. "What I had always known I needed to learn had been the *feel* of things," she says, "all the messy, sticky, slithery side of cooking." *Kitchen Fugue*, the resulting cookbook-autobiography, has humor, charm, and touches of pathos.

In 1943, Sheila engaged with novelist G. B. Stern in a fascinating dialogue about their idol, Jane Austen. *Speaking of Jane Austen* and *More About Jane Austen* are humorous and perceptive conversations, in which the two authors explore every facet of Jane Austen's art, character, and personality.

Sheila Kaye-Smith died on January 14, 1956, with thirty-odd novels to her credit. "A stupendous output by any standard," wrote *The New York Times.* "And not to be dismissed qualitatively because of the quantitive outpouring of her work."

Frank Swinnerton, in *The Georgian Literary Scene,* sees her as the "official novelist" of Sussex. "Sheila Kaye-Smith has made Sussex as much a place of simple passion and pride as Devon or Somerset," he says. "Her novels are models of construction, with the quiet beginning, the natural development of interest, the clean drawing of character, the attainment of a serious warmth of emotion, and sometimes—for she has courage—the climax of death or disaster. Conscience was in them and comment was sent from them. They were dramatic narratives which stood of their own accord as excellent, honorable work."

AGATHA CHRISTIE

[1890–   ]

Undisputed queen of detective story writers, Agatha
Christie was born Agatha Mary Clarissa Miller, youngest
child of an American father and an English mother. Torquay,
her birthplace, is a health resort in South Devon, a civilized
place of parks and pleasure grounds, tennis courts and shaded
bowling greens. Later she would make use of its typically
English scenery as background for her novels. It had pleasant
villas, spanking white yachts on one of the finest sailing
courses in Britain, and nearby villages of genuine antiquity,
with thatched cottages and Norman churches.

As was usual in upper middle class families, Agatha's
brother was packed off to boarding school at an early age. She
and her sister presented more of a problem. At that time, 1890
to about 1905, girls were rarely sent away to school, even
those of exceptional intelligence who thirsted for formal
training. Instead, a succession of nursery maids and governesses was provided for them, ending with a foreign governess who was more of a companion and chaperone than a
teacher. "As education, one had classes," Agatha explains.
"One went to dancing class, Swedish exercises, art school,
piano lessons, singing class, cookery class, etc."

Mrs. Miller had other ideas. To everyone's astonishment,

she despatched Agatha's elder sister to "the Misses Lawrence at Brighton," a pioneer school which later developed into the distinguished boarding school for girls, Roedean. Agatha did not follow her, perhaps because her mother, who could on occasion be delightfully eccentric, had suddenly become convinced that education destroyed a child's brains and ruined her eyesight.

Spared a resident governess, Agatha was tutored by her mother, and most enjoyably. Mrs. Miller read aloud from *Bleak House* and *The Old Curiosity Shop*, arousing in her daughter a passion for Dickens. "I was brought up on Dickens," Agatha once said. "Always loved him, and hated Thackeray. With Dickens you can never tell where the story is going. I always feel with him he got awfully tired of his characters and dragged in more—but the new ones were just as wonderful."

She discovered Milton's *Paradise Lost* for herself. "Of course I didn't understand it, but I loved its sonorous sounds." She loved Jane Austen, too, just as she now loves Elizabeth Bowen, Graham Greene, and Muriel Spark.

Her somewhat desultory education left her with hours of solitude—hours for wandering in the garden, daydreaming, and poring over fairy tales and romances which she later told to any child who came her way.

But her mother, who thought her daughters capable of anything, did not believe in aimless dreaming, even when a child was sick. Finding Agatha in bed with a cold, she ordered her to write a story. "Nonsense! Don't say you can't," she exclaimed. "Of course you can." Eden Philpotts, author of tragic and realistic novels about Devonshire and a friend of the Miller family, visited the young invalid and prodded her gently—so Agatha decided to try. "For some years," she says, "I enjoyed myself very much writing stories of unrelieved gloom where most of the characters died." This enjoyment was to last a lifetime. "None has poured forth a stream of bloodshed comparable to Agatha Christie's," Nigel Dennis wrote some years ago. Wholesale murder is a commonplace in her books. In her novel *And Then There Were None*, every one of the characters comes to a violent end.

Extremely shy as a girl, Agatha took piano and singing lessons in the hope that playing before an audience would give her assurance. But the piano lessons had to be dropped; she was far too nervous to play for others. As a singer, she put in six hours of practice daily, and occasionally performed at amateur concerts. But her voice was not strong enough for opera and she never sang professionally.

At the beginning of World War I, she married Archibald Christie, a handsome young officer in the Royal Flying Corps who was soon called to active duty. Agatha herself joined the Red Cross and worked in a dispensary. She continued to experiment with writing in her leisure time. "I first tried to write poetry. Then a gloomy play—about incest, I think. Then a long, involved, morbid novel—some of the writing wasn't too bad, but the whole thing was pretty poor."

In 1916, a chance remark of her sister's changed the course of her work. "I bet you can't write a good detective story, Agatha," she said. "It must be quite hard."

Agatha rose to the challenge. In imagination she had already constructed innumerable dramas, all of which had their corpses. And she knew something of the methods of detection; she had read Conan Doyle's novels with passionate interest, marveling at the impeccable logic and unfailing aplomb of his Sherlock Holmes.

A model for her own detective was not far to seek. England, at that time, was giving asylum to hundreds of

Belgian refugees, many of whom worked in the neighborhood of Agatha's dispensary. Among them was a prim little man who caught her fancy. Hercule Poirot was born—and in no time at all she had a mystery for him to solve.

She had learned a little about poisons during her hospital work. Now she decided to make use of her knowledge in her story. Feminine in her dislike for guns and knives, she decided that the characters in her detective novels would be killed off with poison. "Give me a nice, deadly phial to play with and I am happy," she would say. And from then on, whenever the plot allowed, she used poison as the murder method.

With little spare time for writing, it took her nearly a year and a half to finish that first novel, *The Mysterious Affair at Styles*. She has long since bettered her speed. "I'm an incredible sausage machine, a perfect sausage machine," she declared to an interviewer. To have a book published in November—the "Christie for Christmas"—she has to deliver the manuscript in March. Actually, she can complete a novel easily in three months, but she prefers to take six or seven, allowing herself time for pleasant interruptions.

The Mysterious Affair at Styles was rejected by several publishers before its acceptance by The Bodley Head. On its appearance in 1920, a crime writer named Sutherland Scott called it "one of the finest novels ever written." Agatha herself was gratified by its reception and quite content with the twenty-five pounds which she received for its use as a serial. She made nothing on the book itself; her contract called for royalties after the sale of 2,500 copies, and only 2,000 were sold.

Book after book followed. Readers became increasingly familiar with Hercule Poirot and his "little grey cells." And they revel in him to this day, a fact which his creator is inclined to deplore. "I can't bear him now," she told Julian

Symons a few years ago. "But he has to go on, because people ask for him so much." She feels that Poirot has become unreal; in England, the private investigator is a rarity.

Although she still cannot dispose of the comical little Belgian, she soon rid herself of his assistant, Captain Hastings. She decided that he was too imitative, too closely modeled upon Sherlock Holmes' friend and assistant, Doctor Watson. Banishing him to the Argentine, she only once recalled him to England. "All my early books were very conventional," she explained once. "They were unnecessarily complicated, with quantities of clues and sub-plots. Stupid policemen were dragged in, and I felt I had to have a detective and a Watson. I got very tired of Captain Hastings."

As a change from Poirot, the author invented another detective, the elderly spinster-sleuth, Jane Marple, now known to many people through the medium of the screen. Like her creator, Miss Marple relishes a murder in quiet family surroundings—"the kind you read about in the paper," says Miss Christie, "not the explosive, gangster type."

Agatha Christie's fourth novel, serialized in a newspaper, brought her five hundred pounds and opened up the most promising vistas. "I bought a thing I thought I would never have," she says. "A car, a bull-nosed Morris. That is one of the big thrills of my life, having a bull-nosed Morris."

With the publication of *The Murder of Roger Ackroyd*, Agatha Christie became the acknowledged "Queen of Crime." This book, her most famous, was a tour de force which kept her huge public guessing. It was later made into a successful play, *Alibi*, although not by Miss Christie, who found the dramatic version unsatisfactory. She could not resign herself to seeing Poirot turn into a young man involved in a sentimental love affair, even though she admitted that Charles Laughton did extremely well in the role.

The success of *Alibi* led to further dramatizations, none of which pleased her. Deciding to dramatize a novel herself, she began with *And Then There Were None*, which became *Ten Little Indians*. She proved to be a natural dramatist and since then there has almost always been a Christie play on the London stage.

Soon after the success of *The Murder of Roger Ackroyd* had made her name known throughout England, Agatha Christie provided the Sussex police with a mystery as baffling as any of her own invention. Her car was found abandoned on the South Downs, and she herself had vanished without a trace.

For two weeks, the missing authoress made headlines. Police with bloodhounds and beagles vainly tried to pick up her trail. Volunteers combed the downs, and farmers lent their tractors to crash through the thickets in search of clues. Airplanes flew low as men trained their binoculars on the chalk hills under them.

Sceptics unkindly dismissed the author's disappearance as a publicity stunt, not knowing that publicity of any kind had always been anathema to her. To this day, she shuns personal appearances, and she looks back with distaste on the extravagant publicity which attended her disappearance.

She was eventually discovered in a Yorkshire hotel, where doctors found her to be suffering from amnesia, brought on by overwork and emotional strain. It has been said of her, admiringly, "Even without her memory, she was able to elude the whole police force." But at the time her readers were deeply concerned, believing that she might never write again.

They were quickly proved wrong. Agatha Christie was soon at work on another of her ingenious and complicated novels. The flow has never halted; in all she has sixty-eight mystery books to her credit, plus six novels written under the pseudonym Mary Westmacott. Seventeen of her plays have been produced. Five are original dramas. Seven are novels dramatized by Agatha herself, while five are Agatha Christie novels dramatized by other authors.

Divorced in 1928, she was able to support herself and her daughter with ease. Not all her time went to her writing; she put equal energy into the sheer enjoyment of living. She swam, listened to Bach, Sibelius, Elgar, and Wagner, collected old furniture and bric-a-brac, and developed a keen interest in decorating. At one time she owned eight houses, all of which she had decorated herself. Today the number is reduced to three—a country house outside a Devonshire village, a house near the Thames, and a flat in London.

Her second marriage, to Max Mallowan, brought a new interest into her life and provided her with new material for her books. A professor of archeology, at one time head of the British School of Archeology in Iraq, he took his wife with him for several months of the year—and gave her the job of cleaning, photographing, and tabulating his finds. As a result, four of her novels are based on archeological work.

Critics have called Agatha Christie's novels "cosmopolitan," largely because some of her best stories have been set on the Continent or in the Middle East. But though she can manipulate her characters equally well on fast trains and river boats, she is most at home in orderly domestic surroundings—villas, cottages, and rectories where the exotic Hercule Poirot stands out with startling effect. "Like suddenly seeing Satan at a Sunday School treat," said one of her fans.

The author herself is apt to be nettled when readers complain that she always sets her books in country houses. "You *have* to be concerned with a house; with where people live," she defends herself. "You can make it a hotel, or a train, or a pub—but it's got to be where people are brought together.

And I think it must be a background that readers will recognize, because explanations are boring. If you set a detective story in, say, a laboratory, I don't think people would enjoy it so much. No, a country house is obviously the best."

Now in her seventies, Agatha Christie lives in a country house not far from Oxford, where her husband lectures on archeology. The house could be one of a hundred such houses in her novels. Untouched by the professional decorator, it is furnished with fine old pieces and is bright with the chintzes that Englishwomen love so well. In the drawing room— dedicated, as are those in her novels, to the ritual of afternoon tea—windows open onto a quiet lawn that stretches down to the Thames.

She is as serenely English as her house. The popular conception of Agatha Christie as a twittering Miss Marple is entirely false. "If she resembles any of her characters," says one of her interviewers, "it is Mrs. Ariadne Oliver, the comfortably cultured matron who occasionally plays second string to Poirot."

She is as happy in her work as she has always been, and as successful. One of her latest novels, *At Bertram's Hotel* (1966), is as compulsively readable as ever, brilliantly characterized and knowledgeably detailed. Currently, she is working on her autobiography, to be published after her death. "I've been rather enjoying jotting down silly little things that happened to me when I was a child," she says. "There'll be a bit about my work, I suppose, not much. If anybody writes about my life in the future, I'd rather they got the facts straight."

Two full-length novels, believed to be among her best, are also being reserved for posthumous publication. "One is Poirot's last case, and one of course Miss Marple's," she explains. "I wrote them during the war, just after *The Body in the Library*, when I was in London, working in hospitals. I had plenty of time in the evenings; one didn't want to go out in the blitz." She has given one to her daughter and one to her husband, "definitely made over to them, by deed of gift." And she adds, characteristically, "So when I am no more they can bring them out and have a jaunt on the proceeds—I hope!"

Posthumous works aside, Miss Christie is venturing on a slightly different type of novel. Her latest book, *Third Girl*, features a coldblooded young thing who grabs all she can get, and a melodramatic burst of violence at the climax. Poirot is the detective in the case, but the author has her doubts about him. "He's not the kind of private eye you'd hire today," she says.

Her readers are not likely to agree; faithful to the urbane little Belgian, they like him precisely as he is.

VICTORIA SACKVILLE-WEST

[1892–1962]

ALTHOUGH MOST writers dream of living in an ivory tower, few are as fortunate as Victoria Sackville-West, who actually achieved one. Visitors to Sissinghurst Castle may see her sitting room in a tower where Queen Elizabeth I once spent three nights. The tower has two turrets, one with a spiral staircase leading to the roof. The other has small, octagonal rooms, in one of which Victoria wrote and studied from 1913 until her death in 1962.

Here are her books, mementoes of her travels, Sackville miniatures, and pictures and manuscripts of her friends. At the back of her writing table are portraits of the people she most loved and admired—her husband, Harold Nicolson; the Brontës; and her intimate friend and fellow writer, Virginia Woolf.

Distinguished poet, novelist, biographer, and critic, Victoria Sackville-West was born March 9, 1892, in Knole, one of the largest "stately homes" of England, situated in Knole Park, Kent. Almost five centuries old, the great house was begun by Thomas Bourchier, archbishop of Canterbury, and enlarged and completed by Thomas Sackville, to whom it was deeded by Queen Elizabeth I. With a passionate love for her home, Vita (as she later called herself) always regretted that she had not been born a boy—a boy who would inherit Knole. It was "like a lover to her," her son Nigel said after her death, "and that is why houses and the idea of inheritance play such an important part in her books." *Knole and the Sackvilles*, which she wrote in 1923, is a narrative of her ancestral home and its occupants.

Her father, the third Baron Sackville, loved and understood his only child. A quiet country gentleman with a distaste for fashionable gatherings, he sympathized with his small daughter when, during week-end parties at Knole, she escaped to the attics to scribble in privacy. Vita was remembering herself when, in *The Edwardians*, she described the young Sebastian's flight to the roof of Chevron. "He had climbed on to the roof not only because for years such exercise had been his favourite pastime but because it was now his only certain method of escape. . . . Sebastian grinned; then he sighed. For the approach of luncheon meant that he must abandon the roof and its high freedom, and the surveying glance it gave him of house, garden and park, and go downstairs to be engulfed once more in the bevy of his mother's guests."

With her mother, Lady Sackville, Vita was ill at ease, feeling that she did not come up to expectation. Lady Sackville was both beautiful and fashionable, a fit subject for John Singer Sargent, the American portrait painter. In later years, her impetuosity developed into an ill-tempered eccentricity that made life difficult for her daughter; she accused Vita and her husband of appalling crimes, tried to alienate their sons, and behaved so outrageously that they refused to accept the allowance which she legally owed them. Nonetheless, the compassionate Vita wrote sympathetically about her mother in *Pepita* (1937), an entrancing story of a romantic episode in the life of her grandfather who, during early manhood, had married a Spanish ballerina. The legality of their marriage was in doubt, and after his death there was a mystery to unravel. Who was the legitimate heir to his historic mansion—the son of his second marriage or the son of the Spanish ballerina? For years, lawyers worked on the problem, tracing witnesses and taking depositions from bullfighters and parish priests in remote corners of Europe. In *Pepita*, Vita Sackville-West told the full and complicated story with warmth, humor, and exquisite clarity.

Vita retained clear and somewhat troubling memories of her childhood at Knole. These are recounted in a brief autobiography which her son, Nigel, found in a locked closet after her death. Her childhood, she supposes, must have been "very much like that of other children." Privileged children, she might have said, for the young Vita had a private park to play in, a summer house where she did her lessons, dogs "absorbingly adored," rabbits, and other pets, and a "little cart" to which she harnessed three of her dogs.

The grown-up Vita is hard on the child; she remembers her as "plain, lean, dark, unsocial, unattractive—horribly unattractive!—rough and secret." Certainly she had masculine traits which she retained throughout her life; she was fiercely independent, impatient of feminine foibles, happiest when she could wear breeches and gaiters and stay close to the earth. But the rough-and-tumble little girl grew into a woman who could be gentle and tolerant, with illimitable patience for those who needed her.

She began to write when she was about twelve, her imagination set afire by *Cyrano de Bergerac*. "I never stopped writing after that," she says, "historical novels, pretentious, quite uninteresting and pedantic, and all written at an unflagging speed; the day after one was finished another would be begun." She had plenty of time to study and write; during her adolescence she fled from social life whenever she could, detested her own sex, and was only occasionally unhappy in her chosen solitude.

As was the custom for English girls of the upper classes, she "came out" when she was eighteen, a procedure which involved presentation before the King and Queen in Buckingham Palace. She was spared the usual round of debutante dances and parties when the death of King Edward VII plunged England into mourning. She did, however, attend one significant dinner party, the one at which she met her future husband, Harold Nicolson, third son of Sir Arthur Nicolson, later Lord Carnock.

She was captivated by him; Harold had a special gift for putting the young and shy at ease. Vita found him "very young, alive and charming. . . . Everything was fun to his energy, vitality and buoyancy." In the following year they became secretly engaged, and soon afterward they were married in the chapel at Knole.

To those who knew them well, they appeared to be utterly unsuited. Vita, her son says, "was anti-social, passionate, romantic, secret and undomesticated. He (Harold) was gay, immensely sociable, ambitious, phil-Hellenistic, and profoundly interested in the ways and politics of the world." Yet their marriage was deeply and enduringly happy, with Vita at first doing her utmost to adapt to the role of diplomat's wife. "I was no longer plain," she says, "I took adequate trouble to make myself agreeable, Harold was loved by everyone who met him—we were, in fact, a nice young couple to ask out to dinner."

Early in their marriage, and with her husband's complete understanding and sympathy, Vita reverted to type. She no longer accompanied him to his posts abroad. From 1915 to 1930, the Nicolsons made their home in Long Barn, a small, fifteenth-century house two miles from Knole, where their sons, Ben and Nigel, were born. (In 1936, when Charles and Anne Lindbergh fled to England to escape the attentions of the Press, they spent two secluded years in Long Barn. Harold Nicolson, telephoning the village postmistress to ask her to see that the Lindberghs were not disturbed, was quickly reassured by the promise, "No, sir, we shall not stare at the poor people.")

Vita, writing endlessly, was reserved and shy, even with her children. Patient with their interruptions, she nonetheless closed the blotter secretively over her work when they burst into her room.

Her first novel, *Heritage*, was published in 1919, and was followed in the early twenties by several other books, among them *Seducers in Ecuador* and *Passenger to Teheran*. In 1927, she won the Hawthornden Prize with her long poem, *The Land*, her most characteristic work. A description of the year's cycle of an English farmer, it is a passionate and somber tribute to the character and beauty of Kent—its history, agriculture, scenery, and people. It was written partly at Long Barn and partly in Persia during two short visits to her husband—visits which provided much of the inspiration for the glorious gardens which she was to design later.

Although she refused to go with him, Vita suffered cruelly from her husband's absences. In 1929, she wrote him a letter which was so heartbreaking that he gave up his diplomatic career and joined the staff of London's *Evening Standard*. From then on, Vita lived with him in London and spent her week ends at Long Barn.

At peace with herself, she began to write *The Edwardians*, a novel based on memories of her girlhood at Knole. An unequaled picture of the "smart set" about 1905, it is a brilliant recreation of a vanished age. One of her best-known novels, it was published by Hogarth Press, owned and directed by Leonard and Virginia Woolf.

Virginia had become the most beloved and important of Vita's few intimates. Their friendship had begun in 1922, when Virginia admired Vita's poems and was eager to read *Knole and the Sackvilles*. It continued through 1923, with Vita dining with the Woolfs in the way she most liked—"No party," Virginia would write, understandingly, "and please don't dress." Soon the two women were exchanging letters and criticisms—and Virginia was hoping that Vita would send Hogarth Press one of her books. Vita had complied with *Seducers in Ecuador*, of which Virginia wrote: "I like its texture—the sense of all the fine things you have dropped in to it, so that it is full of beauty in itself when nothing is happening—nevertheless such interesting things do happen, so suddenly, barely, too. . . . I am very glad we are going to publish it, and extremely proud and touched, with my childlike dazzled affection for you."

Over the years, the friendship deepened into a rare intimacy. So when Virginia needed a subject for her most unusual book, *Orlando*, it was inevitable that she should choose Vita Sackville-West. "Orlando," says Aileen Pippett, one of Virginia's biographers, "was the kind of biography that only Virginia Woolf could write and Vita Sackville-West inspire." In it, the two sides of Vita's nature, the masculine and the feminine, are reflected in the tale of a young nobleman in the 1500's. He has "many adventures in many reigns," yet is still young, vigorous, aristocratic, and a poet—but now a woman —in the year 1928.

In 1930, threatened by encroaching urbanization, the Nicolsons decided to look for another home, one with privacy, beauty, and ground for gardens. Exploring the Weald of Kent and Sussex, they heard about Sissinghurst Castle, a great Tudor and Elizabethan mansion which had slowly fallen to pieces. Vita visited it and fell so much in love with it that they determined to buy it and undertake the colossal task of restoration.

It proved to be a long labor of love. Little survived of the original great house except the South Cottage and the Priest's House, both in a poor state of repair. "There were only vegetable gardens," says the Appendix to Harold Nicolson's *Diaries and Letters*, "and a vast accumulation of rubbish dating back to the occupation of the castle by French prisoners in the mid-eighteenth century. . . . Otherwise nothing but old brick walls, and the moat which had enclosed a medieval house on the same site."

By 1932, the Nicolsons were living in the castle, sometimes under Spartan conditions, Vita and Harold in the South Cottage, and their sons in the Priest's House. "It made an odd house to live in," says the guide to Sissinghurst Castle. "Each person inhabited a separate building, and to sleep, eat, bathe and work meant a walk, summer or winter, across the garden from one part to another. . . . There was no guest room, which struck people as strange for a Castle, but Sissinghurst was never luxurious, nor even very comfortable."

To Vita, the appeal of its neglected gardens was irresistible. "I saw what might be made of it," she wrote in the *Journal of the Royal Horticultural Society*. "It was Sleeping Beauty's Castle; but a castle running away into sordidness and squalor; a garden crying out for rescue." She and her husband spent seven years in the rescue work, and the whole garden was finished by 1937.

In spite of her preoccupation with Sissinghurst, Vita continued to write. Within two years, she followed her successful *The Edwardians* with two other novels, *All Passion Spent* in 1931, and *Family History* in 1932. Her husband called the former "a lovely book" and both it and the moving *Family*

History were well received by both the critics and the reading public.

In 1933, Vita paid her first and last visit to America; her husband was to repeat the journey many times. They made a lecture tour from coast to coast, and from Canada to the deep South, sometimes together but more often separated. Already well known to Americans for their writings, they were enthusiastically received, especially when they appeared together to discuss such subjects as "What We Think about Marriage" or "Changes in English Social Life." In Arizona, where they allowed themselves a holiday, Vita was astounded at the immensity of the Grand Canyon; it was "like nothing on earth." Later, she recaptured her impressions in *Grand Canyon*, published in 1942.

Back in England, Vita returned gladly to Sissinghurst, to carry out her plans for extending the house and gardens. The design of the gardens was her husband's. "I could never have done it myself," she said. "Fortunately I had acquired, through marriage, the ideal collaborator. Harold Nicolson should have been a garden-architect in another life. He has a natural taste for symmetry, and an ingenuity for forcing focal-point or long-distance views where everything seemed against him, a capacity I totally lack." Together they created a seasonal garden, and later a series with predominant colors—orange and yellow for the cottage garden; white for the garden by the Priest's House; dark blue and purple along the north side of the front courtyard.

In the years that followed, Vita went to London as little as possible; she detested the superficiality of society and of "smart" people. "I hate women's shops," she once wrote to her husband. "Also I hate seeing myself in mirrors, and being asked to look at myself. I do so absolutely loathe my own appearance, and to be forced to look at myself in a long mirror is a real distress to me." A needless distress, because Richard Church, a fellow writer and a close neighbor, compared her to one of her own roses. "She, too," he says, "gave the effect of dusky and dewy beauty, impressively handsome."

In 1934, Vita wrote *The Dark Island,* which the critics found "morbid and depressing," and in 1940 a biography of Joan of Arc. Harold Nicolson, himself a fine reviewer, found it "first-rate. . . . The thing is a very brilliant piece of reconstruction upon factual rather than upon imaginative lines. I believe it will be certain of a great triumph."

Now a respected figure in the literary world, Vita Sackville-West was also a figure in the horticultural world, sharing her experiences as a gardener in such books as *Country Notes, In Your Garden, In Your Garden Again, More for Your Garden,* as well as in a weekly gardening column which she wrote for *The Observer.* During the war years, sheep were bred at Sissinghurst and Virginia Woolf was ecstatic over a parcel she received containing "masses and masses of the finest wool." The farm at Sissinghurst was a working farm, and very productive; it yielded wartime luxuries which could be given to friends and the less fortunate without depriving the farm workers. Virginia, on receiving a pound of golden butter, sent rapturous thanks. "You've forgotten what butter tastes like. So I'll tell you—it's between dew and honey."

Vita was prominent in the movement to display the great national gardens of Britain to the public. After the war, the gardens at Sissinghurst were open all year round. Richard Church described them for prospective visitors in an essay in *The Observer.* "Lost and ruined courtyards in the old castle have been converted into sunken gardens, enclosed with tall yew hedges; and these enclosures form the nucleus of the central part of the garden round what survives of the old castle. Beyond them stretch avenues, woodland paths, and glades down to a moat which opens across a herb garden to a vista of the Kentish Weald. Dominating the whole is the old rose-brick tower where the doyenne of the place had her writing-table."

Vita Sackville-West died at Sissinghurst Castle in June of 1962. "Almost my last memory of her," says her son Nigel, "is when I arrived at Sissinghurst one summer evening and she tried to rise from her chair to greet me (me, her son!) only to fall back in exhaustion. Two days later, she died."

She left the Castle and garden to Nigel, with the exception of the South Cottage, which was bequeathed to Harold Nicolson for his lifetime. To posterity she left a body of fine writings and one of the most beautiful gardens in Europe, a place of rare and varied loveliness to visit on a summer's day.

DOROTHY L. SAYERS

[1893–1957]

In an engaging little book on the joys of reading, Burton Rascoe talks about authors and their ways of life and work. "The experience of life need not be violent to make a good author," he says. "Jane Austen lived a quiet and uneventful life and yet managed to attain as high a niche in the hall of fame as was ever accorded to a woman."

He might also have taken Dorothy Sayers as his example. Like Jane Austen, she was the daughter of a clergyman and led an uneventful life. Yet her novels touch on a wide variety of experience and are intimately concerned with violence, murder, and sudden death. When the reader opens *Have His Carcase*, he meets its heroine, Harriet Vane, stumbling over a body as she looks for a picnic spot on the lonely beach at Lesston Hoe. "Harriet's luck was in," the author observes coolly (Harriet, herself a writer of mystery stories, could capitalize on the experience). "It *was* a corpse. Not the sort of corpse where there could be any doubt, either. Mr. Samuel Weare of Lyons Inn, whose 'throat was cut from ear to ear' could not have been more indubitably a corpse. Indeed, if the head did not come off in Harriet's hand, it was only because the spine was intact, for the larynx and all the great vessels of the neck had been severed 'to the hause-bone' and a frightful stream, bright red and glistening, was running over the surface of the rock and dripping into a little hollow below."

A dead body is treated with similar nonchalance in *The Five Red Herrings*, when the Kirkcudbright doctor turns over the corpse of the landscape painter, Campbell. It moved "all of a piece and bundled together, as though it had stiffened in the act of hiding its face from the brutal teeth of the rocks." Its gruesome appearance does not in the least upset Lord Peter Wimsey, detective; he merely laughs and says, "He's got knocked about a bit."

Certainly there was nothing in Dorothy Sayers' quiet, hard-working life to afford material for the plots of such novels as *Strong Poison, Whose Body?* or *Unnatural Death*. By temperament and training she was a scholar, and she spent the first and last years of her life in the scholarly pursuits she loved. She took to detective story writing for the most prosaic of reasons: "I had to make money somehow." In *Gaudy Night*, through the medium of Harriet Vane, she makes it plain just how she feels about her avocation. Harriet, who has returned to her college for a reunion, shrinks from meeting her former friends. "What would those women say to her," she wonders, "to Harriet Vane, who has taken her First in English and gone to London to write mystery fiction?" It is the author speaking, too, when Harriet, studying her reflection, smooths her academic gown and laughs suddenly. "They can't take this away at any rate," she says. "Whatever I may have done since, this remains. Scholar; Master of Arts; Domina; Senior Member of this University . . . a place achieved, inalienable, worthy of reverence."

In 1893, Dorothy Leigh Sayers was born in Oxford, daughter of the Reverend H. Sayers, headmaster of the Cathedral Choir School. She was brought up in the Church of England and took her religion seriously; the struggles between two of its parties, the Anglo-Catholic and the Evangelistic, later challenged her to enter the controversy and write her theological plays and religious essays.

Her mother, Helen May Leigh, was the greatniece of Percival Leigh, the "Professor" of *Punch*, an English weekly first published in 1841 which retains to this day its reputation for satirical humor. Dorothy may well have inherited from this ancestor the dry humor and rapier wit which distinguish both her religious writings and her detective novels.

Her girlhood was spent in East Anglia, the fen country, a seventy-mile tract, originally swampland, where the Romans were first to build roads and attempt drainage in England. In *The Nine Tailors*, Dorothy sets her story in this flat and windswept land, where Lord Peter Wimsey is discovered raging impotently at his overturned car. He soon deduces what has happened. "The narrow, hump-backed bridge, blind as an eyeless begger, spanned the dark drain at right angles, dropping plump down upon the narrow road that crested the dyke. Coming a trifle too fast across the bridge, blinded by the bitter easterly snowstorm, he had overshot the road and plunged down the side of the dyke into the deep ditch beyond, where the black spikes of a thorn hedge stood bleak and unwelcoming."

Many of the picturesque names common in the fen country are used in the book—Jack Priest, Mr. Gotobed, Potty Peake, Hezekiah Lavender, Ezra Wilderspin. The plot is woven around one of Dorothy Sayers' hobbies, campanology; the bells—Gaude, Sabaoth, John, Jericho, Jubilee, Dimity, Batty Thomas, and Tailor Paul—are fatefully involved in a grim mystery. Dorothy Sayers loved bells and bell lore and made this plain in her foreword. "It seems strange that a generation which tolerates the internal combustion engine and the wailing of the jazz band should be so sensitive to the one loud noise that is made to the glory of God," she says. "England, alone in the world, has perfected the art of change-ringing and the true ringing of bells by rope and wheel, and will not lightly surrender her unique heritage."

It was probably inevitable that, when the time came, Dorothy should choose to study in Oxford. That university, together with Cambridge, had the pick of all the young brains in the country. She was fortunate in coming to university-age when she did; women students had been admitted to full membership of the university only a few years earlier. Impressed by its reputation for scholarship, she chose to attend Somerville College, which was named after a formidable woman scholar, mathematician, and physicist.

Somerville gave her congenial companions and all and more than she needed for her intellectual development. She read, and did her research, in Oxford's unique Bodleian library, with its million and a half volumes, its forty thousand manuscripts, its priceless documents about British history and literature. Duly recommended by a don, she was permitted to examine such treasures as the seventh-century manuscript of the *Acts of the Apostles*, used by the Venerable Bede, and Caedmon's *Metrical Translation of Genesis*. Soon she was dreaming and planning the works of scholarship which she herself would undertake.

But Oxford life was not all study. There were the narrow streets to wander through—"the High," "the Turl," "the Corn," and especially the stately "Broad," with its enticing bookstores and the temptation of Blackwell's inviting notice: "When you visit Blackwell's no one will ask you what you want. You are free to ramble where you will; to handle any book; in short, to browse at leisure. . . . Such has been the tradition at Blackwell's for more than seventy years."

There were walks, solitary or companionable, through

green quadrangles and college gardens, each different, each delightful. There was punting on the Char, and excursions along the bank, with a pause for "rural refreshment" at the Trout, an old country inn with river gardens and strutting peacocks. There was first-class cricket to watch in the university parks, and Boar Hill to climb for a view of the city. And there were festivities—the summer balls in the bedecked quadrangles, and the Vice-Chancellor's garden parties, with strawberries and cream on the lawn.

In *Gaudy Night*, one of her finest books, Dorothy Sayers made use of her vivid and loving memories of her college; Shrewsbury is Somerville, thinly disguised. The plot, ingenious and complicated, involves a campaign of terror on a campus that seethes with wrangling and suspicion. The characterization, with its sharply etched portraits of dons and tutors, "old girls" and "scouts," is brilliant. But much of the interest of the book lies in its authentic background of undergraduate life in Oxford; the reader is soon in sympathy with Harriet Vane, as she looks back upon her student days. "One could realize that one was a citizen of no mean city. It might be an old and old-fashioned city, with inconvenient buildings and narrow streets where passersby squabble foolishly about the right of way; but her foundations were set upon the holy hills and her spires touched heaven."

Dorothy Sayers "came down" from Somerville in 1916 with a First in Modern Languages, one of the first women to obtain an Oxford degree. Before she was twenty a small volume of verse, *Op. 1*, was published. This was followed by *Catholic Tales*, short stories which gave an indication of fine things to come.

Settling temporarily in London, she made her living as a copywriter in one of the city's leading advertising agencies. Here she learned to write tight, readable prose, to meet deadlines, to dig up facts and weigh and present them accurately. The experience stood her in good stead when, in 1923, she turned to writing detective novels.

She was not without preparation for this kind of writing. At Oxford she had made a careful, critical study of the craft. Once, in later life, she remarked during a lecture that Aristotle, in his *Poetics*, was obviously hankering after a good detective story. "He had clearly stated that it was the writer's business to lead the reader up the garden, to make the murderer's villainy implicit in his character from the beginning, and to remember that the *dénouement* is the most difficult part of the story."

In *Whose Body?* Dorothy Sayers revitalized the art of the detective story by her lively prose, her contemporary quality, and by her invention of a totally new type of detective in Lord Peter Wimsey. Erudite, astute, Lord Peter hid his talents behind a mask of ineptitude. In a later novel, one of the characters remarks that she has met Lord Peter at a dog show, "giving a perfect imitation of a silly-ass-about-town." No one could give a more convincing picture of effete British aristocracy than Lord Peter Wimsey—but it was camouflage.

Five more novels featuring Lord Peter appeared during the next five years: *Clouds of Witnesses, Unnatural Death, The Unpleasantness at the Bellona Club, The Documents in the Case,* and *Strong Poison.* Then the author's yearning for a more scholarly type of writing made itself felt, and she turned with relief to something completely different. In Oxford, she had done considerable research in medieval literature. Now, out of the fragments of the Anglo-Norman version of the *Roman de Tristan,* she constructed a modern English story, telling it partly in verse and partly in prose.

But as she herself remarked, "There was no very hopeful market in those days for poetry or theology." So she returned to her detective novels and, in *Have His Carcase*, introduced a companion for Lord Peter in the shape of Harriet Vane, a scholarly and highly independent young woman whom her reader suspects to be much like the author herself. By this time, Dorothy was married to Captain Atherton Fleming and could write with insight and humor about "the way of a man with a maid." Henceforth she lets Harriet work with Lord Peter in such bafflers as *Gaudy Night*, and Harriet's struggle to avoid surrendering her independence by marriage to Peter makes an engrossing story-within-a-story.

In *Busman's Honeymoon* (1936), Lord Peter was permitted to marry. Collaborating with M. St. Clair Byrne, Dorothy dramatized the novel in the same year, describing the play as "a love story with detective interruptions." It was so successful that, in 1937, she was asked to write a play for the Canterbury Cathedral Festival. This drama, *The Zeal of Thy House*, was an enlightening, deeply felt study of the purification of an artist in the twelfth century. Acclaimed during the festival, it was also produced in London at His Majesty's Theatre.

Dorothy Sayers did not return to detective-story writing after 1937; indeed, she seems to have felt guilty about the years she had devoted to this type of work. "It would be well to discourage the idea that I am a writer of mystery-fiction, who in middle age suddenly 'got religion' and started to preach the gospel," she once told an interviewer. "The truth is the exact contrary. I was a scholar of my college. . . . Having, in one way or another, made sufficient money to live on, I was able to drop the detective fiction, and go back to the literary criticism, verse-translation, and so on, which I had been trained and qualified to do."

She had no reason to think lightly of her detective novels. Her books are definitely the work of a scholar; from the outset, she insisted upon being informative, although in a humorous way. When she presents the reader with a dozen suspects, they are certain to have peculiar occupations or unusual hobbies—and these must be explored and analyzed before the plot may proceed. Lord Peter is a fount of knowledge. When, in his amiable fashion, he sets to work on a case, he gives the reader not only his deductions about the crime and the criminal but snippets of information about everything from incunabula to vintage wines.

After abandoning her famous detective in 1937, Dorothy Sayers began the task which she regarded as the true purpose of her life—that of making religion real and vivid for the widest public. *The Devil to Pay*, her second play written for the Canterbury Cathedral Festival, is a modern version of the story of Doctor Faustus. Contemporary in plot and expression, it was extraordinarily effective on the stage. She followed it with a cycle of radio plays on the life of Christ, entitled *The Man Born To Be King* and produced by the British Broadcasting Company year after year as its Christmas attraction.

Turning to the essay form, she continued to be both prolific and distinguished. Her belief in God as Creator, her philosophy of life, her judgments on various phases of learning were covered in several volumes, among them *Begin Here*, *The Mind of the Maker*, and *Unpopular Opinions*.

Her greatest scholarly undertaking was a translation of the works of Dante. His natural piety and colloquial idiom had always attracted her; her own religious life was built on natural piety and common sense, supported by extensive reading. Her translations of the *Inferno* and the *Purgatorio* were labors of love but were not wholly successful. "She caught the directness of the original," said one critic, "but failed to catch the poetry. But her prose comments have done more than those of any other recent English author to quicken interest in Dante."

As a measure of relief from this demanding project, she found time to translate the earliest and noblest of the French *chansons de geste*, the *Chanson de Roland*. That completed, she began to translate Dante's third volume, the *Paradiso*. She found this the most difficult, perhaps because her energies were flagging because of failing health.

Dorothy Sayers died of a thrombosis in 1957, having made worthy contributions to English literature in two very different fields. Scholars will remember her for her meticulous translations and her valuable commentary on the work of Dante. The general reader, for whose pleasure her books are continually being reprinted, will be grateful to her for the Wimsey books, classics of the detective novel proper, and especially for Lord Peter himself, aristocrat, dilettante, and detective par excellence.

RUMER GODDEN

[1907–   ]

Novelist, playwright, poet, translator, and author of memorable books for children, Rumer Godden has traveled in three continents and has known many homes. There was her grandmother's dark old house in London, "so quiet that on the top landing one could hear the tick of the grandfather clock in the hall." There was the old house in Narayangunj, where the Godden sisters lived like princesses, "a monstrous house, a great rectangular pale-grey stucco house, standing on a high plinth that was hidden by plumbago and a hedge of poinsettias." There was a farm in Kashmir, and an old house in Sussex which an editor-friend, Annis Duff, remembers as "one of the most beautiful dwelling-places imaginable." Down the years, Rumer has gone back and forth between England and India, loving both intensely, homesick for the one while she was living in the other.

Born in Rye, a seaside town in Sussex, on December 10, 1907, she was taken to India when she was six months old. "Fa," her father, was a steamship agent for the oldest company serving Bihar, Assam, and Bengal. Jon, her elder sister by sixteen months, had been born in Assam, where her parents had lived on a steamer moored to the bank. "Our lives were conditioned by the rivers," Rumer said; "they gave a

sense of proportion, of timelessness, to our small township."
Two other sisters, Nancy and Rose, arrived to round out the
close-knit family.

Fa came of good yeoman stock—"pirates and smugglers, if
you ask me," the children's Aunt Mabel suggested, but with
no discoverable evidence. A strikingly handsome man, he
resembled his great-grandfather, a professor of mathematics
who once went to America to teach at the University of
Virginia. Horrified, he and his wife refused to have servants
when they heard that it meant buying slaves. Fa, with the
same regard for humanity, taught his daughters to respect the
beliefs and customs of others, however strange they might be.
When the small Rumer teased Govind, the head gardener, by
chanting aloud the forbidden name of Ram, Fa delivered a
stinging rebuke. "Gods are God," he said. "Whether he is our
God, or Azad Ali's or Govind's. When you are in someone
else's country, you will respect what they respect—and not
trespass."

Rumer's mother, "Mam," was small, plump, tolerant, and
greatly beloved. She was devoted to her daughters. An aunt
who lived with them insisted that, when they came back from
visiting, Mam would walk faster and faster as they neared
home. Her husband, to the children's delight, used to tell one
of his tallest stories about her. "One night, as Mam slept on
the verandah, as she loved to do, a man-eating tiger came and
seized her, and all Mam said was, 'Eat me quietly and don't
wake the children.' " Mam liked to tell them stories about her
family, the Hingleys, who were Quakers, and of her childhood in the big house on the edge of the Black Country, the
smoky, industrial region of the English Midlands. This story-
telling in the family circle encouraged Rumer to make her
own very early start as a writer. Before she was seven, she had
finished the story of her life.

"Children in India are greatly loved and indulged," Rumer says in the prologue to *Two Under the Indian Sun*, "and we never felt that we were foreigners, not India's own." Mam, with her warmth and liberality, followed the Indian way and let her children grow up naturally. So the small Rumer and Jon met with a shock when, at the ages of 5½ and 7 respectively, they were sent to England to be brought up by paternal grandmother and aunts. The house in Randolph Gardens with its meager yard and city sparrows was chill and uninviting after the warmth and scents of India.

Rumer, clever, imaginative, and impressionable, was far more knowledgeable than the average child. Under the influence of her austere and genuinely holy aunts, she began to write "hymns and odes" that reflected the bitterness of exile. She hated the English weather, the stodgy food, the bulky clothing which she and Jon were made to wear. She fretted under the lack of privacy; in Randolph Gardens the children were never alone, except when they were in bed. Even their prayers were public, said "out loud" to an aunt. "It seemed," Rumer remembers, "an unpardonable intrusion."

Yet the experience was a valuable one for the writer-to-be. There were rules to follow; no toys on Sunday and no talking during lunch (and no finishing everything on your plate, either; something had to be left for "Miss Manners"). Rumer learned discipline—the discipline which, in later years, helped her to get through prodigious amounts of work with apparently effortless serenity. "My grandmother was very, very strict," she told a friend. "She taught me to sit in a straight, hard chair (never in a soft one). At five each afternoon I was washed and dressed and sent downstairs to the drawing-room, where I had to read 'Dombey and Son' to my grandmother, play the piano, or embroider, and especially I had to talk. Which latter chore was perhaps the most valuable lesson of all, as I learned one of the obligations of an individual in society." With such a start, small wonder that Rumer Godden is today a witty talker and an always interested listener, although she says "the things I hate worst are parties."

In 1914, faced by the outbreak of World War I and the threat of zeppelin raids over London, the little Goddens were sent back to their parents in India. After the preliminary strangeness was over, they bloomed rapidly, knowing and feeling that they were at home. They soon became used to the big, bright house, the garden, the ponies, the river, and the native servants who might be Brahmins or Buddhists or Muslims—or, like the ayah and the Goanese gardener, Roman Catholics.

Now in their fifties, Jon and Rumer Godden still remember those five enchanted years in India. Recently, they decided to undertake a fascinating literary task, collaboration on a book describing the experiences they shared as children. Their method of collaboration was difficult, but highly effective. Deciding to use no "I's" but only "we's," they first talked over the shared recollection. Then Jon wrote some parts, and Rumer others. After that, they changed manuscripts and "overwrote rather than rewrote." As their styles were very different, they had to consider both versions to see which one was more appealing. Today, not even Rumer or Jon can tell precisely who wrote each part. But the resulting book, published in 1966, is a brilliant evocation of an unusual childhood.

At the end of the war, the children were again shipped back to England, this time to undergo a purgatory of schooling. Rumer, in particular, was desperately unhappy as, unable to conform, they passed from school to school. Rebellious and wretched, she was unable to write until they found a happier milieu in Moira House, a school in Eastbourne, run on free and progressive lines. Here Rumer was encouraged to write although advised not to try for publication until she was twenty-five.

On leaving school, she turned to her secondary interest and studied ballet in London. So complete and thorough was her training that she was able, on her return to India, to open a dancing school in Calcutta, the first of its kind in India. The work was many sided and congenial; she wrote and produced ballets, designed costumes and scenery, arranged the music, and did the choreography. Once a year, the school gave a ballet that extended from a week to ten days. The last of these included 130 children in the cast, forty of whom were under four years of age. This rich experience was later reflected in Rumer's novel, *A Candle for St. Jude*, the story of a ballet school in London.

But although ballet remains a favorite with her to this day, the desire to write proved irresistible and her first book, *Chinese Puzzle*, was published a year after her marriage, which occurred in 1934. She enjoyed the writing of this book more than any other. The tale of a Chinese man and a white Pekinese, it involved two of her abiding interests— Chinese life and literature, and Pekinese dogs. Ready now to make writing her career, she said, "I shall always be grateful to the educator who made me promise that I would not publish anything before I was twenty-five." Two years later, she wrote *The Lady and the Unicorn*.

When World War II broke out, Rumer Godden was on the continent, finishing her third book, *Black Narcissus*, a hauntingly beautiful story of an English sisterhood isolated in the shadow of the Himalayas. This, and her next book, *Gypsy, Gypsy*, have been translated into Norwegian, Dutch, Danish, Polish, and Italian. *Black Narcissus* was made into a successful film, although too much emphasis was placed on melodramatic incident and not enough on the rare beauty of the background and the strangeness of the atmosphere.

In 1942, *Breakfast with the Nikolides* was published, and in 1946, *The River*, both richly detailed novels about English families in India. A meticulous craftsman, writing with fastidious care, she never produces a hasty piece of work. "I myself," she once said, "am one of those slow writers who take months and many drafts to produce their work. I need, as Stephen Spender says, 'avenues of time, pools of quiet.'" She seldom gets them, but she always makes time for the writer's "perpetual battle with shades of sound and meaning."

In 1949, with her second husband, James Haynes Dixon, and her two schoolgirl daughters, she settled in Buckinghamshire in a seventeenth century cottage, situated between those twin centers of village life, the post office and the bakery. Here she listened to gossip over the hedge, grew roses, bred Pekinese, and shared many and unusual interests with her family—the ballet, herbs, Victorian dolls' houses, and comparative religion, with a particular interest in Hindu philosophy.

The cottage, she tells us, "had a great many wastepaper baskets"—with good reason. Everyone in the family wrote "persistently and continuously," books, plays, poems, scripts, and reviews. Rumer herself turned to poetry and wrote *In Noah's Ark*, a lilting narrative poem which springs from the ancient legend of the flood "when all the world was young and all the trees were green," and Mrs. Noah, "whose price was rubies," set up housekeeping for the animals in the hold of the ark.

In the years that followed, Rumer Godden produced a body of distinguished and varied work. *A Breath of Air* (1951) is a novel with a South Sea setting, a modern *Tempest*.

Mooltiki (1957) is a collection of stories and poems from India. In 1955 she wrote a novel about London street children, *An Episode of Sparrows*, and followed it in 1958 with *The Greengage Summer*, a book about more privileged and articulate English children living in France.

Between 1960 and 1963 she found time to write three delightful books for children; two novels, *China Court* and *The Battle of the Villa Fiorita*; and a translation from the French, the subtly beautiful *Prayers from the Ark*. The second of the novels met with its own adventure in a fire that razed her old Sussex house. Rumer was correcting proofs at the time, and they had to be rescued from the blazing building.

During a railway journey, one of Rumer's editors, Annis Duff, heard two young women discussing *China Court*. They agreed that its author seemed to know as much about domesticity as if she actually ran her own household. "But of course she couldn't possibly," one of them said. "She probably has to have everything done for her, because she needs all her time for her writing."

No such ideal state of affairs existed. Family relationships and domestic and social life were making many demands upon the author. She had known the anxiety of a daughter's serious illness and the joy of a grandchild's arrival. For months she had planned the remodeling of an old house and supervised the work. She had taken care of an ailing mother, and run a household for seven people and occasional guests. "And this she did to perfection," said one of her guests, "never allowing it to crowd out the enjoyment of our time together, but with the appearance of effortless serenity that gives the clue to understanding her enormous capacity for work."

Today, having gone full circle, Rumer Godden is living in Rye, Sussex, in a "comfortable" house. Her life is still full and rich, though less hurried than heretofore. Where her books are concerned, she refuses to rush. "Writers need time to think," she told John Barkham. "Once upon a time writers used quills for writing, and while they sharpened their quills they had time to stop and think. Then came the dip pen, followed by the fountain pen, and now the typewriter and microphone. The time for thinking has been whittled away."

She has traveled in the United States, visiting Boston, and colleges in the Midwest and the South. Everywhere, she found that young writers were being told to speed up on the typewriter. The idea shocks her. "Secretaries can type—anyone can type," she says. "But only the writer can write his books, and he should take his time to do the best he can. . . . The best professional writers of today, the ones with the largest bodies of successful work, all arrived by ignoring attempts to have them speed their output."

Rumer is true to her old loves and interests, but she has developed new hates, one of which is the "wicked tendency" to rob children's books of their words, to limit them and simplify them. "English and American children are born with the richest inheritance of words in the world," she stated in *The Writer*. "Then isn't it a cheat to accustom a child to use only 240 of them? It is like forbidding him to walk or run because others are learning to take their first steps."

She has a deep reverence for words. "Words are in my blood," she says. She sees their values in danger of being lost, and makes a plea for them. "I am not, here, writing of journalists. . . . I am writing of the serious novelist whose book, he hopes, will last for a little span at least, will bear re-reading, even be read over and over, be re-printed, find new editions. That is what every novelist hopes of every novel—but does he earn this love and respect?"

Rumer Godden is one who does.

MARY STEWART

[1916–   ]

ALTHOUGH the literary critic is apt to do less than justice to the work of Mary Stewart, the general reader finds her novels as spellbinding as Charlotte Brontë's *Jane Eyre* or Daphne du Maurier's *Rebecca*. The very titles breathe mystery and romance: *The Moon-spinners, Nine Coaches Waiting, Wildfire at Midnight, This Rough Magic.*

Mary Stewart's novels have placed her on the best-seller list in New York, London, and Paris. More than two million copies are in circulation, a figure which does not include a staggering number in paperback. Yet their author had no thought of publication when she was writing her first book. She was simply making a trial flight. She had already published literary articles and poems; now she was experimenting with something different. It was her husband, Frederick Henry Stewart, who persuaded her to send the finished novel to a publisher.

Mary Florence Elinor was born in 1916 in Sunderland, County Durham, a seaport on the River Weare and the largest shipbuilding town in the world. Her father, the Reverend F. A. Rainbow, was a clergyman of the Church of England. He was, she says, "pure English, from the county of Buckinghamshire." Her mother, born Mary Edith Matthews, belonged to a New England family of pioneer missionaries, who labored in New Zealand; she came of mixed stock, which included Polish, Danish, Irish, Welsh, and German. With such a heritage, it seems inevitable that Mary Stewart should have her head in the clouds—but her feet on the ground.

While Mary and her sister and brother were small, their father was made Vicar of Trimdon, a small agricultural village in which they lived until she was seven. The parish, a poor one, offered little in the way of amusement for children, so they made their own. Mary had three toys which she delighted in, "a little rubber horse, a tin elephant, and a small rubber cat that whistled when you pressed it." There were also pencil stubs, plenty of cheap exercise books—and an attic to hide in. The grown-up Mary still remembers that attic, and how she sat diligently scribbling with her toy menagerie as audience.

As a writer, she made an early start; she could "put words on paper" when she was barely three. Her first stories were about her toy animals; she drew the pictures first and fitted the story to them. She hoped to be an artist, not a writer. Writing came so naturally to her that it did not seem worth bothering about.

She grew up in an atmosphere of family affection, warmth, and encouragement. Her first poem, written when she was seven and artlessly entitled *Teeth*, was published in the parish magazine. When they left Trimdon, her mother saved one of her little daughter's books of poems, realizing that it was an achievement for such a young child.

When Mary was eight, the family moved to Shotton Colliery, an ugly mining village in the same county. Although she remembers it with distaste, it left no trace of resentment in her work; Mary Stewart was never to become an Arnold Bennett or a D. H. Lawrence, writing with ineradicable memories of grimy and squalid surroundings. She was to set her novels in beautiful or exotic places—Corfu, Provence, Delphi, Lebanon.

Her first experience of formal education was shattering. At eight, she was sent to boarding school. "I shall not give the name of my first school," she told an interviewer, "because I was so bitterly unhappy there that I had what amounted to a breakdown at the age of ten." Later, and more happily, she attended Eden Hall in Cumberland and Skellfield School in Yorkshire, the latter a girls' "public school," the equivalent of an American private school.

Intending to become a teacher, she went to Durham University and read English Language and Literature for three years. She then took a year's diploma in education. She graduated with an M.A. degree and first class honors in English, a noteworthy achievement.

During her university years, she was an active, all-round student, president of the Women's Union and the Literary Society, and prominent as both producer and actress in college theatricals. "I have always been rather more interested in the dramatic form than in the novel," she told A. A. Horowitz. "I tend to conceive a story first in terms of setting, characters, theme, rather than plot. . . . I find myself writing from one 'peak moment' to the next."

At the beginning of World War II, she started her teaching career and taught for two years. Then her alma mater invited her to return as a lecturer. "I very happily packed my bags," she says, "and returned to Durham, which I loved. I took lodgings and lectured for four years in English."

This is something of an understatement. Besides lecturing and writing, she worked at night for the Royal Observer Corps, a uniformed civilian organization under the operational control of the Royal Air Force Command. The observers reported the movements of aircraft and gave help by indicating the position of aircraft which had crashed or were in distress. In addition to this patriotic duty, Mary produced plays at the university and found time to ride race horses.

On V. E. Day, she had an extra, personal reason for celebration; at a victory dinner, she met her future husband, Dr. Frederick Stewart, then a lecturer in geology at Durham University. She was supposed to go to work in London on the following day, but the meeting changed her mind. She remained in Durham, and married Dr. Stewart three months later. "It was a quick business," she remembers, "very painless."

After her wedding, she continued as part-time Lecturer in English, both at the university and at a local teachers' training college. Five years of teaching and domesticity found her ready for a change, so she returned to writing. Her first novel, *Madam, Will You Talk?* was accepted with encouraging speed. Set in Provence, it has an engaging heroine, a constantly changing background, and a plot which, though somewhat implausible, is compelling in its pace and excitement.

Thunder on the Right, which followed in 1958, enthralled her readers but, in retrospect, displeases its author. "I'm ashamed of it," she told Roy Lindquist, when he interviewed her for his book, *Counterpoint,* "and I'd like to see it drowned beyond recovery. . . . for some strange reason, I went overboard, splurged with adjectives, all colored purple." She is a little hard on what is a highly readable novel, in which Jennifer, a delightful heroine, joins her admirer in investigating a mysterious death in a convent on the Franco-Spanish border.

Thunder on the Right and its two successors, *Nine Coaches Waiting* (1959) and *Wildfire at Midnight* (1961), established their author as mistress of a new genre. Her novels are peculiarly her own; neither detective, suspense, nor mystery stories, they contain elements of each type. "They're not really mysteries," Mary Stewart says. " 'Entertainments' might be a good word, but it's clumsy. I'd rather just say that I write novels, fast-moving stories that entertain."

Her travels spark most of the ideas for her books. When her husband's research takes him abroad, she accompanies him on trips that vary from the rugged and exciting to the leisurely and peaceful. They may, for example, hitchhike to Marseilles or pay a tranquil visit to Haute-Savoie or the Pyrenees. "Beautiful places and buildings with vivid historical associations set my imagination working," she told John Barkham. "I visit a place with my husband, talk to the people, find out how they live. Then, after I have returned home, I send a handful of characters there and the place itself suggests the kind of thing that would happen to them."

In 1955, she and her husband flew to Greece, a country which so enchanted her that she made several return trips, notably to Corfu, which she made the scene of her favorite book, *This Rough Magic*. Corfu is thought to be the island which Shakespeare had in mind when he wrote *The Tempest*. Mary Stewart took the title of her novel from Prospero's abdication speech, and the *Tempest* theme is woven into her story.

Although prolific, Mary Stewart is a careful rather than a quick writer; she takes anything from twelve to eighteen months to complete a novel, and even then is seldom satisfied with it. A perfectionist, she makes three drafts, first writing the dialogue in dramatic form, exactly as it would be spoken in ordinary conversation, then paring it down for emphasis and vividness. Recently, she has learned to dictate into a tape recorder and *Airs Above the Ground* (1965) was dictated in its entirety.

A tall, handsome woman, friendly and unassuming, Mary Stewart is still surprised by her phenomenal success. "I can sit and talk happily to people about books and authors without realizing that I am myself the author of nine books," she told interviewer John Barkham. "As a matter of fact, it still startles me to see my name on books, or to realize that it means anything to anyone. Yet, judging by the letters I receive from readers, it does."

She and her husband live in the fine old city of Edinburgh, Scotland, where he is Regius Professor of Geology at Edinburgh University. This means that he is holder of a university professorship founded by a king, an enviable distinction. When she is not writing, Mary Stewart plans future trips, gardens, visits with her friends, and enjoys art, music, and the theater. "I want to keep on writing, of course," she says, "a new novel every eighteen months or so, good ones if possible." A superb storyteller and a disciplined craftsman, she is perfectly equipped to realize her ambition.

INDEX

123

INDEX

NORAH SMARIDGE

is the daughter of a sea captain and comes of a long line of seafolk from Devonshire, England. After taking an Honors degree at London University, she came to New York City in 1924 with her family and took writing courses at Columbia University and Hunter College.

Although she has been writing since she was nine, Miss Smaridge has had various occupations. She taught for ten years at Marymount High School and Junior College, Fifth Avenue, New York City, and after that worked briefly in a bookstore and a literary agency to gain experience in the book field. This was followed by eleven years as chief copywriter for the St. Anthony Guild Press.

Now writing full time, Miss Smaridge is at her desk from nine to three, and she says that it is work—but she loves it! She types everything, and has produced light verse, serials, short stories, TV scripts, and teen-age and book columns. Some years ago she began writing for children and young people and now has a number of juvenile and teen-age books to her credit. She has also been successful at translating from the French, which language, as well as Italian, she knows well.

A resident of Upper Montclair, New Jersey, Norah Smaridge has lots of young neighbors—and far too many cats. At present she is housing ten felines. She enjoys traveling, mild gardening, is an omnivorous reader, and jumped at the chance to do a book about England's women novelists, including some of her special favorites, Rumer Godden, Agatha Christie, and Jane Austen.